# STEP BY STEP
# CHINESE
# COOKBOOK

# STEP BY STEP
# CHINESE
# COOKBOOK

## PARRAGON

# Contents

*Photography by Peter Barry*
*Designed by Sally Strugnell*
*Jacket Design by Claire Leighton*
*Typesetting by Julie Smith*
*Edited by Jillian Stewart*
*Recipes by Lalita Ahmed, Carolyn Garner,*
*Moyra Frazer, Judith Ferguson and*
*Frederic Lebain*

*3072*
*© 1993 Coombe Books*
*This edition published in 1993 by Coombe Books for*
*Parragon Book Service Ltd,*
*707 High Street, Finchley, London N12 0BT*
*All rights reserved*
*Printed and bound in Singapore*
*ISBN 1-85813-415-3*

# Introduction

As in any other style of cooking, Chinese food is a symbol of life and good health, forming a central part of family and social activity for many people. To the Chinese family, a meal is therefore about much more that just satisfying a physical need, it is an integral part of their social life.

In Chinese cuisine, the preparation of the food is of paramount importance. Many dishes require very fine chopping and shredding of the various ingredients, and they are combined in a very orderly manner. Those ingredients which are not available in the Western world can be substituted with similar products and alternatives to foods which may be difficult to obtain are given in the recipes. It is not necessary to use only Chinese utensils as many dishes can easily be prepared using basic kitchen equipment.

The main cooking technique used to produce Chinese food is stir-frying. A wok is ideal, but a deep non-stick pan will serve the purpose. Stir-frying requires good temperature control and this is easily learnt through practice. The wok should be heated, then the temperature reduced before adding the cooking oil. If the utensil is too hot the oil will burn, giving a charred, oily taste to the food. The heat should be progressively raised for the addition of other ingredients. The whole process may take between five and seven minutes. The most important thing to remember is to never overcook, as this will not only destroy the crispness of the food, but also its flavour and goodness.

Chinese food incorporates six basic flavours: sweet, sour, salty, spicy, pungent and hot. Their employment and respective proportions must be well balanced. Flavouring is always supplemented by ready-made sauces, the most essential of which is soy sauce.

Finally, garnishing should not be neglected, as presentation is as important as preparation. After all, what appeals to the eye also appeals to the mind and stomach! A slice of cleverly carved carrot, a thin sliver of tomato and carefully arranged parsley or coriander can add that all important dash of colour.

Cooking is always a pleasure, especially Chinese cooking. It is a challenge and a way to explore one's creative talents. In any case, who does not want their efforts rewarded by the pleasure of an exquisite Chinese meal.

# Soups

Peking-Style Soup
Chicken and Asparagus Soup
Turkey Soup with Black Mushrooms
Curry Soup with Meatballs
Eggflower Soup
Crab Soup with Ginger
Chicken Noodle Soup
Bamboo Shoot Soup
Chicken and Mushroom Soup
Wonton Soup
Duck Soup
Sweetcorn and Chicken Soup
Hot and Sour Soup
Crab and Watercress Soup
Noodles in Soup
Chinese Parsley and Fish Soup
Crab and Sweetcorn Soup

# PEKING-STYLE SOUP

*Duck stock is the basis of this tasty, filling soup, which
contains meat and vegetables, and is delicately
flavoured with sesame seeds and soy sauce.*

*SERVES 4*

4 slices smoked ham
1 head Chinese cabbage
850ml/1½ pints duck stock
1 tbsp sesame seeds
Pinch chopped garlic
15ml/1 tbsp soy sauce
½ tsp white wine vinegar
Salt and pepper
1 egg yolk, beaten

**1.** Cut the ham into small, even-sized cubes.

**2.** Cut the Chinese cabbage into small pieces and simmer briskly for 10 minutes in the duck stock.

**3.** Stir in the sesame seeds, garlic, ham, soy sauce, vinegar and salt and pepper to taste.

**4.** Cook for 10 minute over a gentle heat. Using a teaspoon, drizzle the beaten egg yolk into the soup. Serve immediately.

TIME: Preparation takes about 5 minutes and cooking takes approximately 20 minutes.

VARIATION: Replace the smoked ham with a different smoked meat.

WATCHPOINT: The smoked ham is likely to change colour during cooking.

# CHICKEN AND ASPARAGUS SOUP

*This special occasion soup is sure to impress your guests.*

*SERVES 4*

450g/1lb chicken pieces
1 onion, peeled and chopped roughly
1 carrot, chopped roughly
1 stick celery, chopped roughly
4 peppercorns
1ltr/2 pints water
Salt
Pepper
300g/10oz can asparagus pieces

*Garnish*
Chopped parsley

**1.** Remove chicken meat from bones and cut into fine shreds.

**2.** Put chicken bones, onion, carrot, celery, peppercorns and water in wok, and season with salt and pepper. Bring to the boil, reduce heat, and simmer for 30 minutes. Strain and return stock to wok.

**3.** Add chicken shreds, and simmer until chicken is cooked. Add undrained asparagus pieces. Adjust seasoning. Serve sprinkled with chopped parsley.

TIME: Preparation takes 10 minutes, cooking takes 45 minutes.

COOK'S TIP: If you can afford fresh asparagus, it's taste is better than the tinned variety.

# Turkey Soup with Black Mushrooms

*An unusual blend of flavours which makes a tasty, warming soup.*

*SERVES 4*

175g/6oz turkey breast meat
15ml/1 tbsp sesame oil
50g/2oz dried Chinese black mushrooms,
    soaked for 15 minutes in warm water
850ml/1½ pints chicken stock
15ml/1 tbsp soy sauce
1 slice fresh root ginger
Salt and pepper

1. Cut the turkey meat into slices and then into small cubes.

2. Heat the sesame oil in a wok and stir-fry the meat until brown. Remove from the pan and drain off any excess oil.

3. Cook the mushrooms in boiling, salted water for 10 minutes. Rinse and drain well.

4. Place the mushrooms in a saucepan with the stock. Stir in the meat, soy sauce, ginger and salt and pepper to taste.

5. Bring to the boil and then simmer gently for 15 minutes.

6. Remove the slices of ginger just before serving. Serve the soup piping hot.

TIME: Preparation takes about 8 minutes and cooking takes approximately 35 minutes.

SERVING IDEA: Sprinkle the soup with 1 tbsp chopped fresh chives before serving.

WATCHPOINT: Don't forget to remove the slice of ginger before serving.

# CURRY SOUP WITH MEATBALLS

*A hearty soup which is perfect for heating up a cold winter night.*

*SERVES 4*

---

*Meatballs*
225g/8oz lean minced beef
1 clove garlic, crushed
1 onion, peeled and finely chopped
½ tsp salt
½ tsp curry powder, or ¼ tsp curry paste
½ tsp ground cinnamon
½ tsp ground cloves
½ tsp ground pepper
30g/1oz breadcrumbs
1 small egg, lightly beaten

Peanut oil

*Broth*
5g/1 tsp garam masala
5g/1 tsp turmeric
1 onion, peeled and finely chopped
1 tsp curry leaves
570ml/1 pint water
1 clove garlic, crushed
½ cup desiccated coconut, soaked in 1
  cup hot water for 15 minutes.

**1.** Mix together meatball ingredients, and form into small balls about the size of walnuts.

**2.** Heat wok, add oil and, when hot, fry meatballs. When browned well all over, remove with a slotted spoon, and drain on absorbent paper.

**3.** Carefully drain oil from wok. Add 5ml/1 tsp of oil, and fry spices for the broth for 30 seconds.

**4.** Add onion, curry leaves, and garlic, and cook together for 3 minutes.

**5.** Meanwhile, strain coconut in a sieve, press out as much liquid as possible, and discard the pulp.

**6.** Add water and coconut milk to the wok and simmer together for 5 minutes.

**7.** Adjust seasoning. Strain soup and return to wok. Add meatballs and simmer a further 5 minutes. Serve hot.

---

TIME: Preparation takes 30 minutes, cooking takes 20 minutes.

BUYING GUIDE: You will often find curry leaves in jars on the spice counter in supermarkets.

# EGGFLOWER SOUP

*The exotic name of this soup is derived from the
appearance of the egg in the soup.*

*SERVES 4*

400g/14oz can plum tomatoes
15ml/1 tbsp light soy sauce
570ml/1 pint chicken stock
2 eggs, lightly beaten
2 spring onions, chopped finely

1. Drain and chop tomatoes, removing
pips, and reserve juice.

2. Bring soy sauce, tomato juice and stock
to the boil in the wok. Add tomatoes and
half the spring onions, and cook for 2
minutes.

3. Dribble beaten eggs in gradually,
stirring continuously.

4. Serve immediately, sprinkled with
remaining spring onions.

TIME: Preparation takes 10 minutes, cooking takes 10 minutes.

# CRAB SOUP WITH GINGER

*This delicately flavoured soup, with fresh crab and a
hint of ginger, is perfect for serving at a special dinner.*

*SERVES 4*

1 carrot, chopped
1 onion, chopped
½ leek, chopped
1 bay leaf
2 medium-sized crabs
850ml/1½ pints fish stock
1-inch piece of fresh ginger root, chopped
5ml/1 tsp Sake Chinese wine (optional)
Salt and pepper

1. Make a vegetable stock by putting the
carrot, onion, leek and bay leaf into a
saucepan with a large quantity of water.
Bring to the boil and add the crabs. Allow
to boil briskly for 20 minutes or until
cooked.

2. Remove the crabs when cooked and
allow to cool. Once cooled, break of the
pincers and break the joints, cut open the
back and open the claws. Carefully
remove all the crab meat.

3. Bring the fish stock to the boil and add
the ginger, Sake and the crab meat. Boil
for 15 minutes.

4. Check the seasoning, adding salt and
pepper as necessary. Serve very hot.

TIME: Preparation takes about 40 minutes and cooking takes approximately 35 minutes. It
takes about 30 minutes for the crab to cool, before you can comfortably
remove the meat with your fingers.

WATCHPOINT: Allow plenty of time for opening the crab and removing all the meat. If
time does not permit preparing fresh crab, use canned crab meat.

COOK'S TIP: Prepare the soup the day before serving. If allowed to rest overnight, the
flavour of the soup will develop deliciously. Reheat gently just before serving.

# CHICKEN NOODLE SOUP

*A warming soup enhanced by filling noodles.*

*SERVES 6-8*

450g/1lb Shanghai noodles, or very thin
  noodles
30ml/2 tbsps oil
225g/8oz cooked chicken, cubed
175g/6oz Chinese white cabbage or
  ordinary white cabbage, shredded
1.5 ltrs/2½ pints chicken stock

*Seasoning*
½ tsp sugar
½ tsp salt
10ml/2 tsps Shao Hsing wine or dry sherry
  (optional)
½ tsp monosodium glutamate
10ml/2 tsps light soy sauce

**1.** Add the noodles to a large pan of
boiling water. Stir to loosen the bundles
and boil for 4-5 minutes. (The noodles
should be just tender but not
overcooked.) Drain noodles well.

**2.** Meanwhile, heat the oil in the wok and
fry the chicken for 1-2 minutes. Remove
the chicken and then fry the cabbage in
the same oil for 2 minutes.

**3.** Add the seasoning ingredients and stir
fry for 1 minute. Add the chicken and
cook for a further 1-2 minutes until the
cabbage is tender. Add the stock and
bring to the boil.

**4.** Divide noodles among 6-8 warm soup
bowls and add the hot soup. Serve
immediately.

TIME: Preparation takes 10 minutes, cooking takes 10-12 minutes.

COOK'S TIP: Monosodium glutamate just adds that little bit of extra 'bite' to the
flavour of a dish.

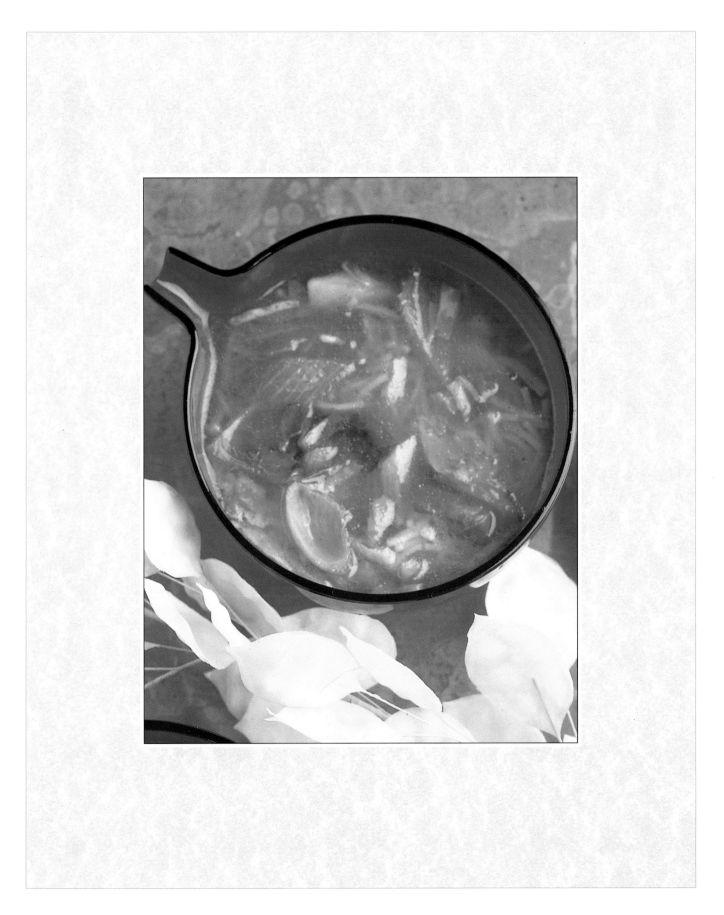

# BAMBOO SHOOT SOUP

*A very decorative soup. Beaten egg sifted into the hot
soup gives a very special effect.*

*SERVES 4*

90g/3oz bamboo shoots, cut into thin
  matchsticks
4 dried Chinese black mushrooms, soaked
  for 15 minutes in warm water
850ml/1½ pints chicken stock
15ml/1 tbsp wine vinegar
30ml/2 tbsps light soy sauce
Salt and pepper
½ tsp cornflour, combined with a little
  water
1 egg
10 chives

1. Blanch the bamboo shoots in boiling,
salted water for 3 minutes. Rinse and set
aside to drain.

2. Cook the mushrooms in boiling, salted
water for 10 minutes. Rinse and set aside
to drain.

3. Bring the stock to the boil and add the
bamboo shoots, mushrooms, vinegar, and
soy sauce and season with salt and
pepper to taste. Cook for 10 minutes.

4. Stir in the cornflour and bring the soup
slowly back to the boil.

5. Reduce the heat. Beat the egg
thoroughly. Place the beaten egg in a
sieve and add to the soup by shaking the
sieve back and forth over the hot soup.

6. Add the chives to the soup and serve
piping hot.

TIME: Preparation takes about 5 minutes and cooking takes approximately 30 minutes.

WATCHPOINT: Make sure the soup is boiling hot before adding the beaten egg.

COOK'S TIP: Try to buy fresh chives for this soup, as they have a
much better flavour than dried chives.

# CHICKEN AND MUSHROOM SOUP

*A classic combination which works well.*

*SERVES 4*

100g/4oz button mushrooms, sliced
50g/2oz dried brown mushrooms, soaked
   and then sliced
50g/2oz dried black mushrooms, soaked
   and then sliced
15ml/1 tbsp oil
1½ litres/2½ pints chicken stock
100g/4oz shredded cooked chicken
3 spring onions, finely chopped
¼ tsp monosodium glutamate (optional)
Salt to taste
15ml/1 tbsp light soy sauce
10ml/2 tsps Shao Hsing wine or dry sherry
   (optional)
Pinch ground white pepper
5g/1 tsp cornflour or arrowroot blended
   with 15ml/1 tbsps stock

**1.** Stir-fry the mushrooms in the oil for 2 minutes and then remove them.

**2.** Bring the stock to the boil in a large pan with the remaining ingredients, apart from the cornflour and mushrooms.

**3.** Add the blended cornflour and the mushrooms, and simmer for 1-2 minutes. Serve immediately.

TIME: Preparation takes 20 minutes, cooking takes 6-8 minutes.

COOK'S TIP: It is well worth hunting for the dried mushrooms as they taste wonderful. They are available in health food stores and Chinese supermarkets.

# WONTON SOUP

*Probably the best-known Chinese soup, this recipe uses
pre-made wonton wrappers for ease of preparation.*

*SERVES 6-8*

20-24 wonton wrappers
90g/3oz finely minced chicken or pork
30g/2 tbsps chopped Chinese parsley
   (coriander)
3 spring onions, finely chopped
2.5cm/1-inch piece fresh ginger, peeled
   and grated
1 egg, lightly beaten
1.5ltrs/2½ pints chicken stock
15ml/1 tbsp dark soy sauce
Dash sesame oil
Salt and pepper
Chinese parsley or watercress for garnish

1. Place all the wonton wrappers on a
large, flat surface. Mix together the
chicken or pork, chopped parsley, spring
onions and ginger. Brush the edges of the
wrappers lightly with beaten egg.

2. Place a small mound of mixture on one
half of the wrappers and fold the other
half over the top to form a triangle.

3. Press with the fingers to seal the edges
well.

4. Bring the stock to the boil in a large
saucepan. Add the filled wontons and
simmer 5-10 minutes or until they float to
the surface.

5. Add remaining ingredients to the soup,
using only the leaves of the parsley or
watercress for garnish.

TIME: Preparation takes 25-30 minutes, cooking takes about 5-10 minutes.

VARIATION: Use equal quantities of crabmeat or prawns to fill the wontons instead of
chicken or pork.

BUYING GUIDE: Wonton wrappers are sometimes called wonton skins. They are available
in speciality shops, delicatessens and Chinese supermarkets. Chinese parsley is also known
as coriander and is available from greengrocers and supermarkets.

# DUCK SOUP

*The perfect start to a Chinese meal,
and it doesn't take too long either.*

*SERVES 4*

2 spring onions, finely chopped
15ml/1 tbsp cooked oil
2.5cm/1-inch fresh root ginger, peeled and
   finely chopped
100g/4oz cooked duck meat, chopped
100g/4oz winter melon, thinly sliced
1½ ltrs/2½ pints chicken stock
Salt to taste
Pinch monosodium glutamate (optional)
15ml/1 tbsp Shao Hsing wine or dry
   sherry (optional)
5ml/1 tsp arrowroot or cornflour blended
   with 15ml/1 tbsp stock
Freshly ground black pepper to taste

1. Fry spring onions in the oil for 1
minute.

2. Add ginger and duck meat. Stir-fry for 1
minute.

3. Add winter melon and stir-fry for a
further 1-2 minutes and then add stock
and the remaining ingredients.

4. Gently simmer for 2-3 minutes until the
soup becomes clear. Serve immediately.

TIME: Preparation takes 10 minutes, cooking takes 8 minutes.

COOK'S TIP: Use the leftovers from a recipe such as Peking Duck for the meat in this recipe.

# SWEETCORN AND CHICKEN SOUP

*A classic soup which is still a great favourite.*

*SERVES 4*

1 chicken, with giblets
225g/8oz can creamy sweetcorn
1 onion, peeled and chopped roughly
1 carrot, scraped and chopped roughly
1 stick celery, chopped
6 peppercorns
Parsley stalks
1 bay leaf
1 ltr/2 pints water
Salt
Pepper

*Garnish*
Chopped parsley or chives

1. Clean chicken, and cut into quarters. Put into wok with giblets, chopped vegetables, peppercorns, bay leaf, parsley stalks, seasoning and water.

2. Bring to the boil. Reduce heat and simmer for 30 minutes. Strain and return stock to wok.

3. Discard the vegetables and giblets. Remove meat from chicken and cut into fine shreds.

4. Add undrained sweetcorn to stock, and bring to boil. Simmer for 5 minutes.

5. Add chicken and cook for 1 minute.

6. Sprinkle with chopped parsley or chives. Serve hot.

TIME: Preparation takes 15 minutes, cooking takes 45 minutes.

# HOT AND SOUR SOUP

*A very warming soup, this is a favourite
in winter in Peking. Add chilli sauce
and vinegar to suit your taste.*

*SERVES 4-6*

60g/2oz pork
3 dried Chinese mushrooms, soaked in
   boiling water for 5 minutes and
   chopped
60g/2oz peeled, uncooked prawns
1.5ltrs/2½ pints chicken stock
30g/1oz bamboo shoots, sliced
3 spring onions, shredded
Salt and pepper
15g/1 tbsp sugar
5ml/1 tsp dark soy sauce
½ tsp light soy sauce
5-10ml/1-2 tsps chilli sauce
25ml/1½ tbsps vinegar
Dash sesame seed oil and rice wine or
   sherry
1 egg, well beaten
30ml/2 tbsps water mixed with 15ml/
   1 tbsp cornflour

**1.** Trim any fat from the pork and slice it
into shreds about 5cm/2 inches long and
less than 5mm/½-inch thick.

**2.** Soak the mushrooms in boiling water
until softened. Place the pork in a large
pot with the prawns and stock. Bring to
the boil and then reduce the heat to allow
to simmer gently for 4-5 minutes. Add all
the remaining ingredients except for the
egg and cornflour and water mixture.
Cook a further 1-2 minutes over low heat.

**3.** Remove the pan from the heat and add
the egg gradually, stirring gently until it
forms threads in the soup.

**4.** Mix a spoonful of the hot soup with the
cornflour and water mixture and add to
the soup, stirring constantly.

**5.** Bring the soup back to simmering point
for 1 minute to thicken the cornflour.
Serve immediately.

TIME: Preparation takes about 25 minutes, cooking takes 7-8 minutes.

PREPARATION: Vary the amount of chilli sauce to suit your own taste.

VARIATION: Hot and Sour Soup is very versatile. Substitute other ingredients such as
chicken, crabmeat, bean sprouts, spinach or green cabbage.

WATCHPOINT: The soup must be hot enough to cook the egg when it is added, but not so
hot that the egg sets immediately.

# CRAB AND WATERCRESS SOUP

*Crab and watercress make a great combination in this quick soup.*

*SERVES 4-6*

1½ ltrs/2½ pints chicken stock
100g/4oz white crab meat, shredded
2 spring onions, finely chopped
2 bunches watercress, finely chopped
Salt and freshly ground black pepper to
    taste
5g/1 tsp cornflour or arrowroot
15ml/1 tbsp water
10ml/2 tsps light soy sauce
A few drops sesame oil

**1.** Bring the stock to the boil with the crab meat, onions and watercress and simmer for 4-5 minutes. Add salt and pepper to taste.

**2.** Mix the cornflour with the water and add to the soup. Allow to simmer for a further 2 minutes.

**3.** Add soy sauce and sesame oil, mix well and simmer for 2 minutes. Serve immediately.

TIME: Preparation takes 10 minutes, cooking takes 8-9 minutes.

BUYING GUIDE: Ensure the watercress is not limp – it deteriorates rapidly once it reaches the supermarket.

# NOODLES IN SOUP

*A simple soup which is nonetheless tasty.*

*SERVES 4-6*

450g/1lb small rounds of noodle cakes
Salt
1.3ltrs/2¼ pints chicken or beef broth, or
   thick stock
100g/4oz cooked shredded chicken
2 eggs, hard boiled and sliced
100g/4oz Chinese napa cabbage, finely
   shredded (or iceberg lettuce)
2 spring onions, thinly sliced

**1.** Cook the noodles in boiling, salted water for 5 minutes. Drain thoroughly.

**2.** Heat the broth or stock and add salt to taste. Serve the cooked noodles in bowls, and pour over the hot broth.

**3.** Garnish with chicken, sliced eggs, cabbage and spring onions, and serve.

TIME: Preparation takes 10 minutes, cooking takes 6-8 minutes.

BUYING GUIDE: Noodles are available in different thicknesses – buy the thinest for soups.

# CHINESE PARSLEY AND FISH SOUP

*Chinese parsley is just another name for coriander,*
*which is available in most good supermarkets.*

*SERVES 4*

450g/1lb white fish fillet, cut into 6 even-
    sized pieces
1ltr/1¾ pints chicken stock
1cm/½-inch fresh root ginger, peeled and
    thinly sliced
Salt to taste
Freshly ground black pepper to taste
Pinch monosodium glutamate (optional)
2 spring onions, finely chopped
½ tsp arrowroot or cornflour
2 sprigs Chinese parsley, finely chopped
18-20 thin cucumber slices

1. Wash fish in cold water and gently
simmer in chicken stock for 2-3 minutes.
Remove the fish pieces carefully.

2. Add ginger, salt, pepper, monosodium
glutamate and spring onion and simmer
the stock for 2-3 minutes. Strain.

3. Dissolve arrowroot in 15ml/1 tbsp water
or cold stock and add to the soup. Simmer
for 2 minutes until the soup thickens.

4. Add fish pieces and bring back to the
boil. Serve in soup bowls, sprinkled with
chopped parsley and cucumber slices.

TIME: Preparation takes 10 minutes, cooking takes 7-8 minutes.

COOK'S TIP: Use your favourite white fish for this recipe.

# CRAB AND SWEETCORN SOUP

*Creamed sweetcorn and succulent crabmeat*
*combine to make a velvety rich soup. Whisked*
*egg whites add an interesting texture.*

*SERVES 4-6*

1ltr/1¾ pints chicken or fish stock
340g/12oz creamed sweetcorn
100g/4oz crabmeat
Salt and pepper
5ml/1 tsp light soy sauce
30g/2 tbsps cornflour
45ml/3 tbsps water or stock
2 egg whites, whisked
4 spring onions for garnish

**1.** Bring the stock to the boil in a large pan. Add the sweetcorn, crabmeat, seasoning and soy sauce. Allow to simmer for 4-5 minutes.

**2.** Mix the cornflour and water or stock and add a spoonful of the hot soup. Return the mixture to the soup and bring back to the boil. Cook until the soup thickens.

**3.** Whisk the egg whites until soft peaks form. Stir into the hot soup just before serving.

**4.** Slice the onions thinly on the diagonal and scatter over the top to serve.

TIME: Preparation takes about 10 minutes, cooking takes about 8-10 minutes.

PREPARATION: Adding the egg whites is optional.

WATCHPOINT: Do not allow the sweetcorn and the crab to boil rapidly; they will both toughen.

ECONOMY: Use crab sticks instead of crabmeat.

VARIATION: Chicken may be used instead of the crabmeat and the cooking time increased to 10-12 minutes.

# Snacks and Starters

Quick-Fried Prawns
Pot Sticker Dumplings
The Peking Duck
Rice Paper Prawn Parcels
Cantonese Egg Fu Yung
Barbecued Spare Ribs
Prawn Fu Yung
Sesame Chicken Wings
Noodles with Ginger and Oyster Sauce
Spring Rolls
Scrambled Eggs with Prawns
Szechuan Bang Bang Chicken
Sesame Prawn Toasts with
Crispy Seaweed
Shanghai Noodles
Steamed Cabbage Rolls with
Fish and Crab-Meat
Mange Tout with Prawns

# QUICK-FRIED PRAWNS

*Prepared with either raw or cooked prawns, this is
an incredibly delicious starter that is extremely easy to cook.*

*SERVES 4-6*

900g/2lbs cooked prawns in their shells
2 cloves garlic, crushed
2.5cm/1-inch piece fresh ginger, finely
　　chopped
15ml/1 tbsp chopped fresh Chinese
　　parsley (coriander)
45ml/3 tbsps oil
15ml/1 tbsp rice wine or dry sherry
25ml/1½ tbsps light soy sauce
Chopped spring onions to garnish

1. Shell the prawns except for the very tail
ends. Place the prawns in a bowl with the
remaining ingredients, except for the
garnish, and leave to marinate for 30
minutes.

2. Heat the wok and add the prawns and
their marinade. Stir-fry briefly to heat the
prawns.

3. Chop the onions roughly or cut into
neat rounds. Sprinkle over the prawns to
serve.

TIME: Preparation takes about 30 minutes for the prawns to marinate.
Cooking takes about 2 minutes.

WATCHPOINT: Do not overcook the prawns as they will toughen.

VARIATION: If uncooked prawns are available, stir-fry with their marinade
until they turn pink.

# POT STICKER DUMPLINGS

*So called because they are fried in very little oil,
they will stick unless they are brown and crisp
on the bottom before they are steamed.*

*MAKES 12*

*Dumplings*
175g/6oz plain flour
½ tsp salt
45ml/3 tbsps oil
Boiling water

*Filling*
100g/4oz finely minced pork or chicken
4 water chestnuts, finely chopped
3 spring onions, finely chopped
½ tsp five spice powder
15ml/1 tbsp light soy sauce
5g/1 tsp sugar
5ml/1 tsp sesame oil

1. Sift the flour and salt into a large bowl and make a well in the centre. Pour in the oil and add enough boiling water to make a pliable dough. Add about 60ml/4 tbsps water at first and begin stirring with a wooden spoon to gradually incorporate the flour. Add more water as necessary. Knead the dough for about 5 minutes and allow to rest for 30 minutes.

2. Divide the dough into 12 pieces and roll each piece out to a circle about 15cm/6 inches in diameter.

3. Mix all the filling ingredients together and place a mound of filling on half of each circle. Fold over the top and press the edges together firmly. Roll over the joined edges using a twisting motion and press down to seal.

4. Pour about 2.5mm/⅛ inch of oil in a large frying pan, preferably cast iron. When the oil is hot, add the dumplings flat side down and cook until nicely browned.

5. When the underside is brown, add about 90ml/3 fl oz water to the pan and cover it tightly.

6. Continue cooking gently for about 5 minutes, or until the top surface of dumplings is steamed and appears cooked. Serve immediately.

TIME: Preparation takes about 50 minutes including the standing time for the dough. Cooking takes about 10-20 minutes.

PREPARATION: The pan used for cooking must have a flat base. Do not use a wok.

WATCHPOINT: Make sure the dumplings are brown and crisp on the bottom before adding the water otherwise they really will be pot stickers!

49

# The Peking Duck

*A magnificent recipe much loved by all fans of Chinese cooking.*

*SERVES 6*

1 duck, weighing 4lbs
½ medium cucumber
4 spring onions

*Sauce*
Small can yellow bean sauce
45g/3 tbsps sugar
30ml/2 tbsps oil

**1.** Clean and dry the duck. Leave in a cool place overnight.

**2.** Finely shred the cucumber and spring onions.

**3.** Preheat the oven to 200°C/400°C/Gas mark 6. Place the duck on a grill rack set on top of a baking pan. Cook the duck for 1¼ hours. The duck should be very dark and crispy.

**4.** For the sauce, heat 2 tbsps oil in a small pan. Add the yellow bean paste and sugar. Cook together for 1-2 minutes.

**5.** Peel the skin off the duck and cut into 2-inch slices. Serve on a heated platter. Carve the meat off the duck into 2-inch slices, serve on a separate platter.

**6.** The duck skin and meat are eaten by wrapping them in pancakes which are first of all brushed with a teaspoon of duck sauce and a layer of cucumber and spring onions.

TIME: Preparation takes about 15 minutes, cooking takes nearly 2 hours.

BUYING GUIDE: More and more supermarkets are stocking a wide range of Chinese sauces, such as yellow bean.

# RICE PAPER PRAWN PARCELS

*The perfect nibble for a drinks party.*

*MAKES ABOUT 20 PARCELS*

225g/8oz prawns, shelled and de-veined
1 egg white
½ tsp cornflour
5ml/1 tsp Chinese wine, or 10ml/2 tsps
   dry sherry
5g/1 tsp sugar
5ml/1 tsp light soy sauce
6 spring onions, finely sliced
Salt
Pepper
140ml/¼ pint peanut oil
1 packet rice paper

1. Dry prepared prawns on absorbent paper.

2. Mix egg white, cornflour, wine, sugar, soy sauce, spring onions and seasoning together. Mix in prawns.

3. Heat peanut oil in wok until hot.

4. Wrap five or six prawns in each piece of rice paper.

5. Gently drop in rice paper parcels and deep fry for about 5 minutes. Serve hot.

TIME: Preparation takes 15 minutes, cooking takes 15 minutes.

# CANTONESE EGG FU YUNG

*As the name suggests, this dish is from Canton.*
*However, fu yung dishes are popular in*
*many other regions of China, too.*

*SERVES 2-3*

5 eggs
50g/2oz shredded cooked meat, poultry
    or fish
1 stick celery, finely shredded
4 Chinese dried mushrooms, soaked in
    boiling water for 5 minutes
50g/2oz bean sprouts
1 small onion, thinly sliced
Pinch salt and pepper
5ml/1 tsp dry sherry
Oil for frying

*Sauce*
15g/1 tbsp cornflour dissolved in 45ml/3
    tbsps cold water
280ml/½ pint chicken stock
5ml/1 tsp tomato ketchup
15ml/1 tbsp soy sauce
Pinch salt and pepper
Dash sesame oil

1. Beat the eggs lightly and add the
shredded meat and celery.

2. Squeeze all the liquid from the dried
mushrooms. Remove the stems and cut
the caps into thin slices. Add the the egg
mixture along with the bean sprouts and
onion. Add a pinch of salt and pepper and
the sherry and stir well.

3. Heat a wok or frying pan and pour in
about 60ml/4 tbsps oil. When hot,
carefully spoon in about 90ml/3 fl oz of
the egg mixture.

4. Brown on one side, turn gently over
and brown the other side. Remove the
cooked patties to a plate and continue
until all the mixture is cooked.

5. Combine all the sauce ingredients in a
small, heavy-based pan and bring slowly
to the boil, stirring continuously until
thickened and cleared. Pour the sauce
over the Egg Fu Yung to serve.

TIME: Preparation takes 25 minutes, cooking takes about 5 minutes for the patties and 8
minutes for the sauce.

VARIATION: Use cooked shellfish such as crab, shrimp or lobster, if desired. Fresh
mushrooms may be used instead of the dried ones. Divide mixture in half or in thirds and
cook one large patty per person.

ECONOMY: Left-over cooked meat such as beef, pork or chicken can be used as an
ingredient.

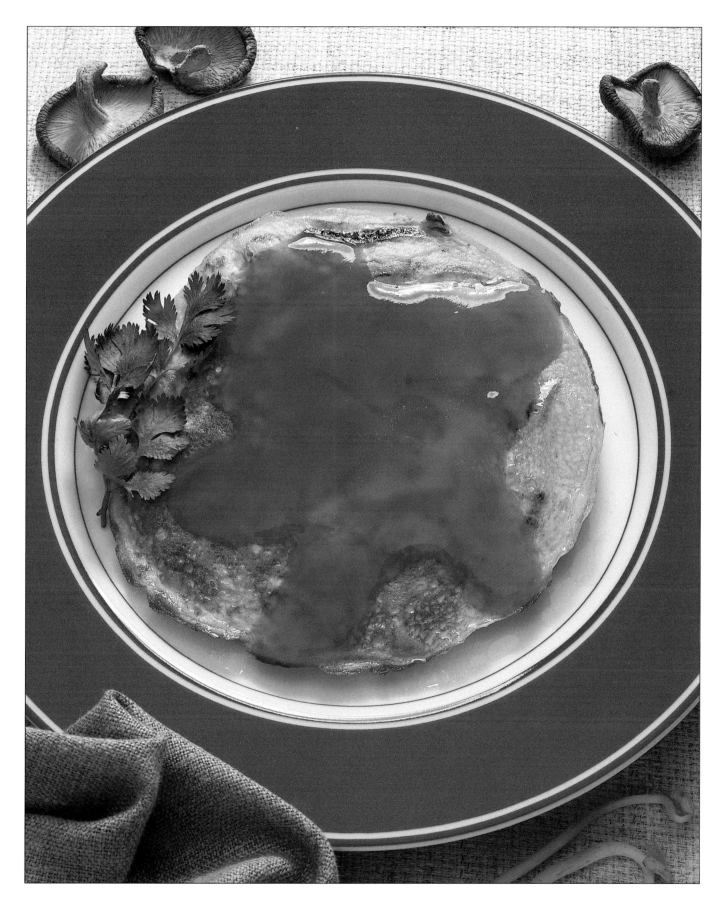

# BARBECUED SPARE RIBS

*Although Chinese barbecue sauce is nothing like
the tomato-based American-style sauce, these ribs
are still tasty cooked on an outdoor grill.*

*SERVES 6-8*

1.8kg/4lbs fresh spare-ribs
45ml/3 tbsps dark soy sauce
90ml/6 tbsps Hoisin sauce
30ml/2 tbsps dry sherry
¼ tsp five spice powder
15g/1 tbsp brown sugar
4-6 spring onions for garnish

1. First prepare the garnish. Trim the root ends and the dark green tops from the onions.

2. Cut both ends into thin strips, leaving about 1.25cm/½ inch in the middle uncut.

3. Place the onions in ice water for several hours or overnight for the ends to curl up.

4. Cut the spare-ribs into one-rib pieces. Mix all the remaining ingredients together, pour over the ribs and stir to coat evenly. Allow to stand for 1 hour.

5. Put the spare-rib pieces on a rack in a roasting pan containing 570ml/1 pint water and cook in a preheated 180°C/ 350°F/Gas Mark 4 oven for 30 minutes. Add more hot water to the pan while cooking, if necessary.

6. Turn the ribs over and brush with the remaining sauce. Cook 30 minutes longer, or until tender. Serve garnished with the onion brushes.

TIME: Preparation takes about 45 minutes. The onion brushes must soak for at least 4 hours and the ribs must marinate for 1 hour. Cooking takes about 1 hour.

PREPARATION: If the ribs are small and not very meaty, cut into two-rib pieces before cooking, then into one-rib pieces just before serving.

COOK'S TIP: The ribs may be prepared in advance and reheated at the same temperature for about 10 minutes.

# SHRIMP FU YUNG

*This dish is perfect for lunch or an evening snack.*

*SERVES 4-6*

Oil
1-2 cloves of garlic, chopped
100g/4oz prawns, peeled
100g/4oz green beans, sliced
1 carrot, shredded
6 eggs
Salt and freshly ground black pepper to
  taste
225ml/8 fl oz chicken stock
¼ tsp salt
10ml/2 tsps soy sauce
5ml/1 tsp sugar
5ml/1 tsp cornflour

1. Heat 30ml/2 tbsps oil in a wok. Add the garlic and stir-fry for 1 minute.

2. Add the prawns and stir-fry for 1 minute.

3. Add the beans and carrots and stir-fry for 2 minutes. Remove and keep on one side.

4. Beat the eggs with salt and pepper to taste, and add the cooled shrimp mixture.

5. Clean the wok and heat 5ml/1 tsp oil. Pour 60ml/4 tbsps of the egg mixture and cook like a pancake. When the egg is set, turn the pancake over and cook on the other side until lightly golden. Place on a warm platter and keep warm.

6. To make the sauce beat the stock with the other sauce ingredients and stir over a gentle heat until the sauce thickens. Serve the pancakes with this sauce.

TIME: Preparation takes 10 minutes, cooking takes 4 minutes for filling/
3-4 minutes for each pancake.

# SESAME CHICKEN WINGS

*This is an economical starter that is also good as a
cocktail snack or as a light meal with stir-fried vegetables.*

*SERVES 8*

12 chicken wings
15g/1 tbsp salted black beans
15ml/1 tbsp water
15ml/1 tbsp oil
2 cloves garlic, crushed
2 slices fresh ginger, cut into fine shreds
45ml/3 tbsps soy sauce
25ml/1½ tbsps dry sherry or rice wine
Large pinch black pepper
15g/1 tbsp sesame seeds

**1.** Cut off and discard the wing tips. Cut between the joint to separate into twin pieces.

**2.** Crush the beans and add the water. Leave to stand.

**3.** Heat the oil in a wok and add the garlic and ginger. Stir briefly and add the chicken wings. Cook, stirring, until lightly browned, about 3 minutes. Add the soy sauce and wine and cook, stirring, about 30 seconds longer. Add the soaked black beans and pepper.

**4.** Cover the wok tightly and allow to simmer for about 8-10 minutes. Uncover and turn the heat to high. Continue cooking, stirring until the liquid is almost evaporated and the chicken wings are glazed with sauce.

**5.** Remove from the heat and sprinkle on sesame seeds. Stir to coat completely and serve. Garnish with spring onions or Chinese parsley, if desired.

TIME: Preparation takes about 25 minutes, cooking takes about 13-14 minutes.

WATCHPOINT: Sesame seeds pop slightly as they cook.

COOK'S TIP: You can prepare the chicken wings ahead of time and reheat them. They are best reheated in the oven for about 5 minutes at 180°C/350°F/Gas Mark 4.

SERVING IDEA: To garnish with spring onion brushes, trim the roots and green tops of spring onions and cut both ends into thin strips, leaving the middle intact. Place in ice water for several hours or overnight for the cut ends to curl up. Drain and use to garnish.

# NOODLES WITH GINGER AND OYSTER SAUCE

*Noodles stir-fried with ginger, carrot and courgettes,*
*then served in an oyster sauce.*

*SERVES 4*

225g/8oz Chinese noodles
1 carrot
1 courgette
3 slices fresh ginger root
1 spring onion, cut into thin rounds
15ml/1 tbsp oil
15ml/1 tbsp soy sauce
30ml/2 tbsps oyster sauce
Salt and pepper

1. Cook the noodles in boiling, salted water, rinse them under cold water, and set aside to drain.

2. Cut the carrot into thin strips. Thickly peel the courgette to include a little of the flesh and cut into thin strips. Discard the centre of the courgette.

3. Peel the fresh ginger root sparingly, but remove any hard parts. Slice thinly, using a potato peeler. Cut the slices into thin strips, using a very sharp knife.

4. Heat the oil in a wok, and stir-fry the spring onion for 10 seconds; add the carrot, courgette and ginger, and stir-fry briefly.

5. Stir in the noodles and cook for 1 minute.

6. Stir in the soy and oyster sauces, and continue cooking until heated through. Season with salt and pepper and serve.

---

TIME: Preparation takes about 15 minutes and cooking takes approximately 15 minutes.

VARIATION: Cook the noodles in chicken stock instead of salted water to give them extra flavour.

COOK'S TIP: Stir-fry the ginger and the other vegetables very quickly, to avoid browning them. Lower the heat if necessary.

# SPRING ROLLS

*One of the most popular Chinese hors d'oeuvres,*
*these are delicious dipped in sweet-sour sauce.*

*MAKES 12*

*Wrappers*
100g/4oz strong plain flour
1 egg, beaten
Cold water

*Filling*
225g/8oz pork, trimmed and finely
    shredded
100g/4oz prawns, shelled and chopped
4 spring onions, finely chopped
10g/2 tbsps chopped fresh ginger
100g/4oz Chinese leaves, shredded
100g/4oz bean sprouts
15ml/1 tbsp light soy sauce
Dash sesame seed oil
1 egg, beaten

1. To prepare the wrappers, sift the flour into a bowl and make a well in the centre. Add the beaten egg and about 15ml/1 tbsp cold water. Begin beating with a wooden spoon, gradually drawing in the flour from the outside to make a smooth dough. Add more water if necessary.

2. Knead the dough until it is elastic and pliable. Place in a covered bowl and chill for about 4 hours or overnight.

3. When ready to roll out, allow the dough to come back to room temperature. Flour a large work surface well and roll the dough out to about 5mm/¼-inch thick.

4. Cut the dough into 12 equal squares and then roll each piece into a larger square about 15 x 15cm/6 x 6 inches. The dough should be very thin. Cover while preparing the filling.

5. Cook the pork in a little of the frying oil for about 2-3 minutes. Add the remaining filling ingredients, except the beaten egg, cook for 2-3 minutes and allow to cool.

6. Lay out the wrappers on a clean work surface with the point of each wrapper facing you. Brush the edges lightly with the beaten egg.

7. Divide the filling among all twelve wrappers, placing it just above the front point. Fold over the sides like an envelope.

8. Fold over the point until the filling is completely covered. Roll up as for a Swiss roll. Press all the edges to seal well.

9. Heat the oil in a deep fat fryer or in a deep pan to 190°C/375°F. Depending upon the size of the fryer, place in 2-4 spring rolls and fry until golden brown on both sides. The rolls will float to the surface when one side has browned and should then be turned over. Drain thoroughly on paper towels and serve hot.

TIME: Preparation takes about 50 minutes for the wrapper dough, the filling and for rolling up. Dough must be allowed to rest for at least 4 hours before use. Cooking takes about 20 minutes.

# Scrambled Eggs with Prawns

*Fish-flavoured scrambled eggs, cooked with prawns*

*SERVES 4*

12 prawns, peeled
8 eggs, beaten
½ stick celery, cut into small dice
1 spring onion, chopped
5ml/1 tsp fish sauce
Salt and pepper

1. Cut the prawns into small pieces.

2. Stir the prawns into the eggs and add the celery, spring onion and fish sauce.

3. Season with a little salt and pepper.

4. Cook by stirring over a gentle heat. When cooked to your liking, serve immediately.

TIME: Preparation takes about 10 minutes and cooking takes approximately 10 minutes.

WATCHPOINT: The fish sauce is very salty. Only add more salt after cooking, if necessary.

# SZECHUAN BANG BANG CHICKEN

*This is a good dish to serve as a starter.*

*SERVES 2*

2 chicken breasts
1 medium cucumber

*Sauce*
60g/4 tbsps peanut butter
10ml/2 tsps sesame oil
½ tsp sugar
¼ tsp salt
10ml/2 tsps stock
½ tsp chilli sauce

1. Simmer the chicken in a pan of water for 30 minutes. Remove the chicken breasts and cut them into ½-inch thick strips.

2. Thinly slice the cucumber. Spread cucumber on a large serving platter. Pile the shredded chicken on top.

3. Mix the peanut butter with the sesame oil, sugar, salt and stock. Pour the sauce evenly over the chicken.

4. Sprinkle the chilli sauce evenly over the top.

TIME: Cooking takes about 30 minutes, final preparation takes 5 minutes.

# SESAME PRAWN TOASTS WITH CRISPY SEAWEED

*Have great fun trying to eat crispy seaweed with your chopsticks!*

*SERVES 2-4*

100g/4oz pork fat
175g/6oz cooked prawns
1 egg white
Salt and pepper to taste
15g/1 tbsp cornflour
2 slices white bread
90g/6 tbsps sesame seeds
Oil for deep frying

*Crispy Seaweed*
2lbs greens
60g/4 tbsps split almonds
Oil for deep frying
½ tsp salt
7.5g/1½ tsps sugar

1. Finely chop pork fat and prawns. Blend together well with egg white, salt, pepper and cornflour. Spread the 'paste' thickly on the 2 slices of bread. Remove the crusts.

2. Sprinkle the paste thickly with sesame seeds pressing them on well.

3. Heat the oil. Lower one slice of bread at a time into the hot oil, spread side down, for 2 minutes. Turn over and fry the other side for ½ minute. Repeat for other slice of bread.

4. Cut each prawn toast in half, then into finger sized strips.

5. With a very sharp knife, cut the greens into the finest shreds possible. Dry, by spreading them out on kitchen paper for ½ hour. Deep fry, or shallow fry the almonds until golden. Drain well.

6. Heat the oil until it is about to smoke. Remove from the heat for ½ minute.

7. Add all the shreds of greens. Stir and return pan to the heat and fry for 2-3 minutes. Remove and drain well.

8. Serve the prawn toasts and crispy seaweed on a well heated platter, sprinkle crispy seaweed evenly with salt, sugar, and almonds.

TIME: Preparation takes 10 minutes for the prawn toasts and 5 minutes for the seaweed, cooking takes about 10 minutes for the prawn toasts and about 3 minutes for the crispy seaweed.

BUYING GUIDE: Sesame seeds can be bought from health food stores as well as some good supermarkets.

# SHANGHAI NOODLES

*In general, noodles are more popular in northern and eastern*
*China, than in other parts of the country. Noodles make*
*a popular snack in Chinese tea houses.*

*SERVES 4*

45ml/3 tbsps oil
100g/4oz chicken breasts
450g/1lb thick Shanghai noodles
100g/4oz Chinese leaves
4 spring onions, thinly sliced
30ml/2 tbsps soy sauce
Freshly ground black pepper
Dash sesame oil

**1.** Heat the oil in the wok and add the chicken cut into thin shreds. Stir-fry for 2-3 minutes.

**2.** Meanwhile, cook the noodles in boiling salted water until just tender – about 6-8 minutes. Drain in a colander and rinse under hot water. Toss in the colander to drain and leave to dry.

**3.** Add the shredded Chinese leaves and spring onions to the chicken in the wok along with the soy sauce, pepper and sesame oil. Cook about 1 minute and toss in the cooked noodles. Stir well and heat through. Serve immediately.

TIME: Preparation takes about 10 minutes, cooking takes 6-8 minutes.

VARIATION: Pork may be used instead of the chicken. Add fresh spinach, shredded, if desired and cook with the Chinese leaves.

BUYING GUIDE: Shanghai noodles are available in Chinese supermarkets and also some delicatessens. If unavailable, substitute tagliatelle or dried Chinese noodles.

# STEAMED CABBAGE ROLLS WITH FISH AND CRAB-MEAT

*This dish can be served as a starter for four people
or as a main dish for two.*

*SERVES 4*

8 large Chinese cabbage leaves
225g/½lb filleted white fish
2 slices ginger root
1½ tsps salt
1 egg white
5ml/1 tsp sesame oil
225g/½lb crab meat

1. Pour boiling water over the cabbage to soften. Drain and dry well.

2. Chop the fish coarsely. Finely chop the ginger. Place the fish and ginger in a bowl with the salt, egg white, sesame oil and crab meat. Mix well.

3. Place 2 cabbage leaves on a flat surface. Put fish mixture into the centre of each of the leaves. Roll the leaves up to form a tight roll.

4. Repeat until all the fish mixture has been used.

5. Insert the fish rolls into a steamer. Steam vigorously for 10-12 minutes. Place the cooked rolls on a heated platter and serve with soy sauce, and chilli sauce as dips.

TIME: Preparation takes about 15 minutes, cooking takes 10-12 minutes.

BUYING GUIDE: If you cannot obtain fresh crab meat use the tinned variety.

# MANGE TOUT WITH PRAWNS

*Snow peas, peapods and mange tout are all names for the same vegetable –*
*bright green, crisp and edible, pods and all.*

*SERVES 2-4*

45ml/3 tbsps oil
50g/2oz split blanched almonds, halved
100g/4oz mange tout
10g/2 tsps cornflour
10ml/2 tsps light soy sauce
175ml/6 fl oz chicken stock
30ml/2 tbsps dry sherry
Salt and pepper
50g/2oz bamboo shoots, sliced
450g/1lb cooked, peeled prawns

1. Heat the oil in a wok. Add the almonds and cook over moderate heat until golden brown. Remove from the oil and drain on paper towels.

2. To prepare the mange tout, tear off the stems and pull them downwards to remove any strings. If the mange tout are small, just remove the stalks. Add the mange tout to the hot oil and cook for about 1 minute. Remove and set aside with the almonds.

3. Drain all the oil from the wok and mix together the cornflour and the remaining ingredients, except the prawns and bamboo shoots. Pour the mixture into the wok and stir constantly while bringing to the boil. Allow to simmer for 1-2 minutes until thickened and cleared.

4. Stir in the prawns and all the other ingredients and heat through for about 1 minute. Serve immediately.

TIME: Preparation takes about 10 minutes, cooking takes 6-8 minutes.

VARIATION: If using spring onions, celery or water chestnuts, cook with the mange tout.

WATCHPOINT: Do not cook the prawns too long or on heat that is too high –
they toughen quite easily.

# Fish and Seafood

Singapore Fish
Cantonese Prawns
Szechuan Fish
Prawns and Ginger
Prawns in Hot Sauce
Sweet-Sour Fish
Honey Sesame Prawns
Steamed Prawn
Whiting Fritters with Cold Fish Sauce
Prawns with Broccoli
Szechuan Fish Steak
Crispy Fish with Chilli
Seafood Chow Mein
Kung Pao Prawn with Cashew Nuts

# SINGAPORE FISH

*The cuisine of Singapore was much influenced by that of
China. In turn, the Chinese introduced ingredients
like curry powder into their cuisine.*

*SERVES 4*

450g/1lb white fish fillets
1 egg white
15g/1 tbsp cornflour
10ml/2 tsps white wine
Salt and pepper
Oil for frying
1 large onion, cut into 1.25cm/½-inch
  thick wedges
15ml/1 tbsp mild curry powder
1 small can pineapple pieces, drained and
  juice reserved, or ½ fresh pineapple,
  peeled and cubed
1 small can mandarin orange segments,
  drained and juice reserved
1 small can sliced water chestnuts, drained
15g/1 tbsp cornflour mixed with juice of 1
  lime
10g/2 tsps sugar (optional)
Pinch salt and pepper

1. Starting at the tail end of the fillets, skin
them using a sharp knife.

2. Slide the knife back and forth along the
length of each fillet, pushing the fish flesh
along as you go.

3. Cut the fish into even-sized pieces,
about 5cm/2 inches.

4. Mix together the egg white, cornflour,
wine, salt and pepper. Place the fish in the
mixture and leave to stand while heating
the oil.

5. When the oil is hot, fry a few pieces of
fish at a time until light golden brown and
crisp. Remove the fish to paper towels to
drain, and continue until all the fish is
cooked.

6. Remove all but 15ml/1 tbsp of the oil
from the wok and add the onion. Stir-fry
the onion for 1-2 minutes and add the
curry powder. Cook the onion and curry
powder for a further 1-2 minutes. Add the
juice from the pineapple and mandarin
oranges and bring to the boil.

7. Combine the cornflour and lime juice
and add a spoonful of the boiling fruit
juice. Return the mixture to the wok and
cook until thickened, about 2 minutes.
Taste and add sugar if desired.

8. Add the fruit, water chestnuts and fried
fish to the wok and stir to coat. Heat
through 1 minute and serve immediately.

TIME: Preparation takes about 25 minutes, cooking takes about 10 minutes.

VARIATION: Chicken may be used in place of the fish and cooked in the same way.
Garnish with Chinese parsley leaves if desired.

SERVING IDEA: Serve with plain rice, fried rice or cooked Chinese noodles.

# CANTONESE PRAWNS

*This quick and easy recipe is suitable for those
times when unexpected friends drop in for lunch.*

*SERVES 2-3*

45ml/3 tbsps oil
2 cloves garlic, finely crushed
450g/1lb peeled prawns
5cm/2 inch root ginger, peeled and finely
    chopped
100g/4oz uncooked pork or bacon, finely
    chopped

*Sauce*
15ml/1 tbsp rice wine or dry sherry
15ml/1 tbsp light soy sauce
5g/1 tsp sugar
225ml/8 fl oz stock or water
15g/1 tbsp cornflour mixed with 30ml/
    2 tbsps stock or water

2-3 spring onions, chopped
2 eggs, lightly beaten

**1.** Heat 1 tbsp oil in a wok. Add the garlic
and fry for 1 minute.

**2.** Add the prawns and stir-fry for 4-5
minutes. Remove to a dish. Keep warm.

**3.** Add the remaining oil to the wok and
fry the ginger and pork for 3-4 minutes
until it loses its colour.

**4.** Add the mixed sauce ingredients to the
wok and cook for 1 minute.

**5.** Add the onions and cook for 1 minute.
Add the beaten eggs and cook for 1-2
minutes, without stirring, until it sets.
Spoon the egg mixture over the prawns.

**6.** Alternatively, add the prawns along
with the beaten eggs. Allow the eggs to
set and then mix gently. Serve at once.

TIME: Preparation takes 10 minutes, cooking takes 15 minutes.

COOK'S TIP: Dry sherry is always a good substitute for Chinese wine so keep a bottle
specially for this purpose.

# SZECHUAN FISH

*The piquant spiciness of Szechuan pepper is quite
different from that of black or white pepper. Beware,
though, too much can numb the mouth temporarily!*

*SERVES 6*

6 red or green chilli peppers
450g/1lb white fish fillets
Pinch salt and pepper
1 egg
75g/5 tbsps flour
90ml/6 tbsps white wine
Oil for frying
60g/2oz cooked ham, cut in small dice
2.5cm/1-inch piece fresh ginger, finely
　　diced
½-1 red or green chilli pepper, cored,
　　seeded and finely diced
6 water chestnuts, finely diced
4 spring onions, finely chopped
45ml/3 tbsps light soy sauce
5ml/1 tsp cider vinegar or rice wine
　　vinegar
2.5cm/½ tsp ground Szechuan pepper
　　(optional)
280ml/½ pint light stock
15g/1 tbsp cornflour dissolved with 30ml/
　　2 tbsps water
10g/2 tsps sugar

1. To prepare the garnish, choose
unblemished chilli peppers with the stems
on. Using a small, sharp knife, cut the
peppers in strips, starting from the pointed
end.

2. Cut down to within 1.25cm/½ inch of
the stem end. Rinse out the seeds under
cold running water and place the peppers
in iced water.

3. Leave the peppers to soak for at least 4
hours or overnight until they open up like
flower.

4. Cut the fish fillets into 5cm/2-inch
pieces and season with salt and pepper.
Beat the egg well and add flour and wine
to make a batter. Dredge the fish lightly
with flour and then dip into the batter.
Coat the fish well.

5. Heat a wok and when hot, add enough
oil to deep-fry the fish. When the oil is
hot, fry a few pieces of fish at a time, until
golden brown. Drain and proceed until all
the fish is cooked.

6. Remove all but 15ml/1 tbsp of oil from
the wok and add the ham, ginger, diced
chilli pepper, water chestnuts and spring
onions. Cook for about 1 minute and add
the soy sauce and vinegar. If using
Szechuan pepper, add at this point. Stir
well and cook for a further 1 minute.
Remove the vegetables from the pan and
set them aside.

7. Add the stock to the wok and bring to
the boil. When boiling, add 1 spoonful of
the hot stock to the cornflour mixture.
Add the mixture back to the stock and
reboil, stirring constantly until thickened.

8. Stir in the sugar and return the fish and
vegetables to the sauce. Heat through for
30 seconds and serve at once.

TIME: Preparation takes about 30 minutes. Chilli pepper garnish takes at least 4 hours to
soak. Cooking takes about 10 minutes.

# PRAWNS AND GINGER

*An age-old combination which has stood the test of time.*

*SERVES 4*

30ml/2 tbsps oil
675g/1½lbs peeled prawns
2.5cm/1 inch fresh root ginger, peeled and
    finely chopped
2 cloves garlic, peeled and finely chopped
2-3 spring onions, chopped lengthways
    into 2.5cm/1-inch pieces
1 leek, white part only, cut into strips
100g/4oz shelled peas
175g/6oz bean sprouts

*Seasoning*
30ml/2 tbsps dark soy sauce
5g/1 tsp sugar
Pinch monosodium glutamate (optional)
Pinch of salt

**1.** Heat the oil in a wok and stir-fry the prawns for 2-3 minutes. Remove the prawns to a dish.

**2.** Reheat the oil and add the ginger and garlic and fry for 1 minute.

**3.** Add the onions and stir-fry for 1 minute.

**4.** Add the leek, peas and bean sprouts. Fry for 2-3 minutes.

**5.** Sprinkle over the seasoning ingredients and return the prawns to the wok. Cover and cook for 20 minutes. Serve immediately.

TIME: Preparation takes 10 minutes, cooking takes 10 minutes.

BUYING GUIDE: Always buy bean sprouts on the day your intend to use them, as they deteriorate rapidly.

# PRAWNS IN HOT SAUCE

*A quick dish that is perfect for a mid-week treat.*

*SERVES 2*

350g/12oz cooked shelled prawns

*Seasoning*
5ml/1 tsp malt vinegar
5ml/1 tsp Shao Hsing wine or dry sherry
Pinch salt

*Sauce*
5g/1 tsp cornflour mixed with 1 tbsp water
10ml/2 tsps tomato purée
Salt and freshly ground black pepper to taste
10g/2 tsps sugar
½ tsp monosodium glutamate (optional)
5ml/1 tsp hot chilli sauce
175ml/6 fl oz chicken stock

30ml/2 tbsps cooked oil
1 onion, chopped
1 stick celery, sliced
1 clove garlic, peeled and crushed

1. Wash prawns and drain well. Mix the seasoning ingredients together.

2. Mix the sauce ingredients together in a separate bowl.

3. Heat the oil in a wok and deep-fry the prawns for 1 minute. Remove the prawns and drain. Keep the oil.

4. Reheat the wok and add 10ml/2 tsps oil and stir-fry the onion, celery and garlic for 1 minute.

5. Add prawns and blended sauce ingredients. Bring to the boil and simmer gently for 3-4 minutes. Stir in the seasoning mixture.

TIME: Preparation takes 10 minutes, cooking takes 6 minutes.

# SWEET-SOUR FISH

*In China this dish is almost always prepared with freshwater
fish, but sea bass is also an excellent choice.*

*SERVES 2*

1 sea bass, grey mullet or carp, weighing
   about 900g/2lbs, cleaned
15ml/1 tbsp dry sherry
Few slices fresh ginger
100g/4oz sugar
90ml/6 tbsps cider vinegar
15ml/1 tbsp soy sauce
30g/2 tbsps cornflour
1 clove garlic, crushed
2 spring onions, shredded
1 small carrot, peeled and finely shredded
30g/1oz bamboo shoots, shredded

1. Rinse the fish well inside and out. Make three diagonal cuts on each side of the fish with a sharp knife.

2. Trim off the fins, leaving the dorsal fin on top.

3. Trim the tail to two neat points.

4. Bring enough water to cover the fish to boil in a wok. Gently lower the fish into the boiling water and add the sherry and ginger. Cover the wok tightly and remove at once from the heat. Allow to stand 15-20 minutes to let the fish cook in the residual heat.

5. To test if the fish is cooked, pull the dorsal fin – if it comes off easily the fish is done. If not, return the wok to the heat and bring to the boil. Remove from the heat and leave the fish to stand a further 5 minutes. Transfer the fish to a heated serving dish and keep it warm.

6. Take all but 60ml/4 tbsps of the fish cooking liquid from the wok. Add the remaining ingredients including the vegetables and cook, stirring constantly, until the sauce thickens. Spoon some of the sauce over the fish to serve and serve the rest separately.

TIME: Preparation takes about 25 minutes, cooking takes about 15-25 minutes.

COOK'S TIP: The diagonal cuts in the side of the fish ensure even cooking.

VARIATION: If desired, use smaller fish such as trout or red mullet and shorten the cooking time to 10-15 minutes.

PREPARATION: The fish may also be cooked in the oven in a large roasting pan or in greased foil sprinkled with sherry. Cook at 190°C/375°F/Gas Mark 5 for 10 minutes per 1.25cm/½-inch thickness, measured around the middle of the fish.

# Honey Sesame Prawns

*Prawns sweetened with honey and sprinkled*
*with sesame seeds – the perfect dish to spoil yourself with.*

*SERVES 4*

100g/4oz self-raising flour
Pinch of salt
Pepper
1 egg, lightly beaten
140ml/¼ pint water
450g/1lb prawns shelled and de-veined
30g/2 tbsps cornflour
Oil for deep frying
15ml/1 tbsp sesame oil
30g/2 tbsps honey
15g/1 tbsp sesame seeds

1. Sift flour and salt and pepper into a bowl. Make a well in the centre, add egg and water, and gradually mix in the flour.

2. Beat to a smooth batter and set aside for 10 minutes.

3. Meanwhile, toss prawns in cornflour and coat well. Shake off any excess cornflour. Add prawns to batter and coat well.

4. Heat oil in wok and add prawns, a few at a time. Cook until batter is golden. Remove prawns, drain on absorbent paper, and keep warm. Repeat until all prawns have been fried.

5. Carefully remove hot oil from wok. Gently heat sesame oil in pan.

6. Add honey and stir until mixed well and heat through. Add prawns to mixture and toss well.

7. Sprinkle over sesame seeds and again toss well. Serve immediately.

TIME: Preparation takes 20 minutes, cooking takes 20 minutes.

# STEAMED PRAWNS

*Fresh prawn, garnished with courgette peel, steamed
and served with a fish-flavoured sauce.*

*SERVES 4*

15ml/1 tbsp fish sauce
5ml/1 tbsp water
15ml/1 tbsp wine vinegar
15ml/1 tbsp soy sauce
10g/2 tsps sugar
10 fresh mint leaves, finely chopped
1 shallot, chopped
Salt and pepper
12 fresh prawns, peeled and cleaned
2 medium-sized courgettes, peeled and
  the peel cut into long strips

1. Mix together the fish sauce, water,
vinegar, soy sauce, sugar, mint, shallot
and salt and pepper. Stir well and set
aside for a least 1 hour.

2. Just before serving time, season the
prawn with plenty of salt and pepper.

3. Roll the strips of courgette peel around
the prawns and cook them in a Chinese
steamer for 5 minutes.

4. Serve the prawn piping hot,
accompanied with the sauce.

TIME: Preparation takes about 20 minutes and cooking takes about
10 minutes for 2 batches.

COOK'S TIP: If the strips of courgette peel are not very pliable, blanch them in boiling
water for 3 seconds, before wrapping around the prawn.

WATCHPOINT: The sauce can be prepared just before cooking the prawn, but it is much
tastier if prepared at least 1 hour in advance.

# WHITING FRITTERS WITH COLD FISH SAUCE

*The delicate flavour of mint in this recipe adds a refreshing taste.*

*SERVES 4*

175g/6oz self-raising flour, sifted
5g/1 tsp baking powder
60ml/2 fl oz water
1 egg, beaten
5ml/1 tsp oil
450g/1lb whiting fillets
Salt and pepper
Oil for deep frying

*For the sauce*
15ml/1 tbsp fish sauce
15ml/1 tbsp soy sauce
15ml/1 tbsp fish stock
Few leaves fresh mint, finely chopped

1. Make the batter by mixing together the sifted flour and the baking powder.

2. Mix in the water, followed by the egg.

3. Add the oil and a good pinch of salt and beat all the ingredients together well. Set the batter aside to rest for a few minutes.

4. Season the whiting fillets with salt and pepper and cut them into small strips.

5. Heat the oil for deep-frying. Dip the whiting strips into the batter and fry them in the hot oil until crisp and golden.

6. Remove the fritters and drain them on paper towels. Keep hot.

7. Meanwhile, mix together the sauce ingredients and serve with the hot whiting fritters.

TIME: Preparation takes about 15 minutes and cooking takes approximately 20 minutes, as you will need to fry the fritters in several batches.

VARIATION: If you do not have the sauce ingredients, the fritters are delicious with a little lemon juice.

COOK'S TIP: Make the sauce a few hours in advance. This gives the flavour of the mint time to develop.

# PRAWNS WITH BROCCOLI

*This dish is also suitable as a starter in small quantities.*

*SERVES 4*

450g/1lb peeled prawns
Oil for deep frying

*Sauce*
100ml/4 fl oz chicken stock
10g/2 tsps cornflour
Freshly ground black pepper and salt to taste
Pinch monosodium glutamate (optional)
5g/1 tsp sugar

*Seasoning*
30ml/2 tbsps cooked oil, or oil from deep frying the prawns
Pinch salt
½ tsp sugar
Pinch monosodium glutamate (optional)
10g/2 tsps cornflour

250g/8oz broccoli cut into 8cm/3-inch pieces
1 carrot, peeled and sliced
2 cloves garlic, peeled and chopped
1cm/½ inch fresh root ginger, peeled and chopped

1. Deep-fry the prawns in hot oil for 1-2 minutes. Drain the prawns and keep to one side. Keep the oil.

2. Mix the sauce ingredients together. Mix the seasoning ingredients together in a separate bowl.

3. Cook the broccoli in boiling water for 1 minute. Drain and add cold water to cover. Drain once again and mix the broccoli with the seasoning ingredients.

4. Heat the wok and add 30ml/2 tbsps cooked oil. Add the carrot, garlic and ginger and stir-fry for 1 minute. Add the broccoli and stir-fry for 1 minute more.

5. Add the prawns and stir-fry for ½ minute then add the blended sauce ingredients. Cook gently until the sauce thickens. Serve immediately.

TIME: Preparation takes 10 minutes, cooking takes 8-10 minutes.

# SZECHUAN FISH STEAK

*Szechuan food is hot and this recipe makes a wonderfully zippy fish dish.*

*SERVES 4*

675g/1½lbs haddock
10g/2 tsps salt
30g/2 tbsps cornflour
1 egg

*Sauce*
1 large onion
2 cloves garlic
3 slices ginger root
2 chilli peppers
2 slices Szechuan Ja Chai pickle (see
   Cook's Tip)
1 dried chilli
Oil for deep frying
90ml/6 tbsps chicken stock
45ml/3 tbsps soy sauce
30g/2 tbsps tomato paste
30ml/2 tbsps Hoisin sauce
15g/1 tbsp sugar
15ml/1 tbsp wine vinegar
30ml/2 tbsps pale sherry

1. Cut fish into 2 x 1-inch oblong pieces. Rub with salt. Blend the cornflour with the egg. Dip the fish in the egg mixture to coat on both sides.

2. Thinly slice the onion. Finely chop the garlic, ginger, chillies, pickle and dried chilli.

3. Heat 4 tbsps oil in a large frying pan. Add the onion and other chopped vegetables; stir-fry for 2 minutes.

4. Add the stock, soy sauce, paste, Hoisin sauce, sugar, vinegar, and sherry. Stir them over a high heat until well reduced.

5. Heat about 4 cups oil in a deep fryer. When hot, add the fish and fry for 2 minutes. Remove and drain.

6. Place them in the pan of sauce. Simmer in the sauce for 5 minutes before serving.

TIME: Preparation takes 10 minutes, cooking takes 10 minutes.

COOK'S TIP: If you cannot obtain the Ja Chai pickle, substitute your favourite hot pickle.

# CRISPY FISH WITH CHILLI

*Choose your favourite white fish for this recipe.*

*SERVES 4*

450g/1lb fish fillet, skinned, bones removed, and cut into 2.5cm/1-inch cubes

*Batter*
60g/2oz plain flour
1 egg, separated
15ml/1 tbsp oil
75ml/5 tbsps milk
Salt
Oil for deep frying

*Sauce*
5g/1 tsp grated root ginger
¼ tsp chilli powder
30g/2 tbsps tomato purée
30g/2 tbsps tomato chutney
30ml/2 tbsps dark soy sauce
30ml/2 tbsps Chinese wine or dry sherry
30ml/2 tbsps water
5g/1 tsp sugar

1 red chilli, seeds removed, and sliced finely
1 clove garlic, crushed
Salt
Pepper

1. Sift the flour with a pinch of salt. Make a well in the centre, and drop in the egg yolk and oil.

2. Mix to a smooth batter with the milk, gradually incorporating the flour. Beat well. Cover and set aside in a cool place for 30 minutes.

3. Whisk egg white until stiff, and fold into batter just before using.

4. Heat oil in wok. Dip fish pieces into batter and coat completely. When oil is hot, carefully lower fish pieces in until cooked through and golden brown – about 10 minutes. Remove with a slotted spoon.

5. Reheat oil and refry each fish piece for 2 minutes. Remove with a slotted spoon and drain on absorbent paper.

6. Carefully remove all but 15ml/1 tbsp of oil from the wok.

7. Heat oil, add chilli, ginger, garlic, chilli powder, tomato purée, tomato chutney, soy sauce, sugar, wine and water, and salt and pepper to taste.

8. Stir well over heat for 3 minutes. Increase heat and toss in fish pieces. Coat with sauce and, when heated through, serve immediately.

TIME: Preparation takes 40 minutes, cooking takes 30 minutes.

COOK'S TIP: Choose your favourite type of fish for this recipe.

# SEAFOOD CHOW MEIN

*Chinese noodles cooked with mussels, cockles and
vegetables and served in a rich ginger
and wine flavoured sauce.*

*SERVES 4*

225g/8oz Chinese noodles
½ green pepper, seeded
½ red pepper, seeded
15ml/1 tbsp oil
½ tsp chopped garlic
½ tsp chopped fresh ginger root
½ spring onion, chopped
125g/5oz uncooked mussels (shelled)
50g/2oz uncooked cockles (shelled)
15ml/1 tbsp Chinese wine
30ml/2 tbsps soy sauce
Salt and pepper

1. Cook the noodles in boiling, salted
water. Rinse them under cold water and
set aside to drain.

2. Cut the peppers into thin slices.

3. Heat the oil in a wok and stir-fry the
garlic, ginger, peppers and spring onion
for 1 minute.

4. Stir in the mussels, cockles, Chinese
wine, soy sauce and the cooked noodles.

5. Mix together well, using chopsticks.
Season with salt and pepper and serve
when cooked through completely.

TIME: Preparation takes about 15 minutes and cooking takes approximately 15 minutes.

VARIATION: Add other types of seafood to this dish.

WATCHPOINT: In Step 5 heat the noodles thoroughly, turning
them in the sauce, to coat evenly.

# KUNG PAO PRAWN WITH CASHEW NUTS

*It is said that Kung Pao invented this dish, but
to this day no one knows who he was!*

*SERVES 6*

½ tsp chopped fresh ginger
5g/1 tsp chopped garlic
25g/1½ tbsps cornflour
¼ tsp bicarbonate of soda
Salt and pepper
¼ tsp sugar
450g/1lb uncooked prawns
60ml/4 tbsps oil
1 small onion, cut into dice
1 large or 2 small courgettes, cut into
    1.25cm/½-inch cubes
1 small red pepper, cut into 1.25cm/½-
inch cubes
60g/2oz cashew nuts

*Sauce*
175ml/6 fl oz chicken stock
15g/1 tbsp cornflour
10ml/2 tsps chilli sauce
10ml/2 tsps bean paste (optional)
10ml/2 tsps sesame oil
15ml/1 tbsp dry sherry or rice wine

1. Mix together the ginger, garlic, 25g/1½ tbsps cornflour, bicarbonate of soda, salt, pepper and sugar.

2. If the prawns are unpeeled, remove the peels and the dark vein running along the rounded side. If large, cut in half. Place in the dry ingredients and leave to stand for 20 minutes.

3. Heat the oil in a wok and when hot add the prawns. Cook, stirring over high heat for about 20 seconds, or just until the prawns change colour. Transfer to a plate.

4. Add the onion to the same oil in the wok and cook for about 1 minute. Add the courgettes and red pepper and cook about 30 seconds.

5. Mix the sauce ingredients together and add to the wok. Cook, stirring constantly, until the sauce is slightly thickened. Add the prawns and the cashew nuts and heat through completely.

TIME: Preparation takes about 20 minutes, cooking takes about 3 minutes.

VARIATION: If using cooked prawns, add with the vegetables. Vary amount of chilli sauce to suit your taste.

SERVING IDEA: Serve with plain or fried rice.

# Meat

Pork and Prawn Chow Mein

Lamb with Tomatoes

Sweet and Sour Beef

Pork Spare Ribs

Beef with Broccoli

Fillet Steak Chinese Style

Pork with Green Peppers

Five-Spice Beef with Broccoli

Beef with Onions

Sweet and Sour Pork

Spiced Beef

Meat and Prawn Chow Mein

Sweet and Sour Pork and Pineapple

Stir-fry Beef with Mango Slices

Lamb Meatballs with Yogurt

Caramelised Spareribs

Beef with Green Pepper and Chilli

Beef Steak with Ginger

Pork Meat Balls in Sauce

Peking Beef

Lamb Curry

Sweet Pork with Vegetables

Braised Hong Kong Beef

Beef with Green Beans

Diced Pork with Walnuts

Beef with Tomato and Pepper in Black
Bean Sauce

Steamed Lamb with Mushroom Sauce

Pork with Black Bean Sauce

# PORK & PRAWN CHOW MEIN

*Chinese chow mein dishes are usually based on noodles,
using more expensive ingredients in small amounts.
This makes economical everyday fare.*

*SERVES 4-6*

225g/8oz medium dried Chinese noodles
Oil
225g/8oz pork fillet, thinly sliced
1 carrot, peeled and shredded
1 small red pepper, cored, seeded and
    thinly sliced
90g/3oz bean sprouts
60g/2oz mange tout
15ml/1 tbsp rice wine or dry sherry
30ml/2 tbsps soy sauce
100g/4oz peeled, cooked prawns

1. Cook the noodles in plenty of boiling
salted water for about 4-5 minutes. Rinse
under hot water and drain thoroughly.

2. Heat the wok and add oil. Stir-fry the
pork 4-5 minutes or until almost cooked.
Add the carrots to the wok and cook for
1-2 minutes.

3. Add the red pepper and add the
remaining vegetables, wine and soy sauce.
Cook for about 2 minutes.

4. Add the cooked, drained noodles and
prawns and toss over heat for 1-2 minutes.
Serve immediately.

TIME: Preparation takes about 20 minutes. The noodles take 4-5 minutes to cook
and the stir-fried ingredients need to cook for about 5-6 minutes for the pork and about
3 minutes for the vegetables.

VARIATION: Use green pepper instead of red, or add other vegetables such as
baby corn ears, mushrooms or peas.

BUYING GUIDE: Dried Chinese noodles are available in three thicknesses. Thin noodles
are usually reserved for soup, while medium and thick noodles are used for fried dishes.

# LAMB WITH TOMATOES

*Lamb and tomatoes make a wonderful,
if unusual, combination.*

*SERVES 2*

10g/2 tsps cornflour
½ tsp salt
15ml/1 tbsp light soy sauce
60ml/4 tbsps water
45ml/3 tbsps oil
1cm/½ inch fresh root ginger, sliced
225g/½lb lamb fillet, cut across the grain
   in thin strips of 1 x 5cm/½ x 2 inches
2 spring onions, chopped
1 onion, peeled and cut into 2.5cm/1-inch
   pieces
1 green pepper, seeded and cut into strips
5g/1 tsp curry powder
3-4 small, firm tomatoes, cut into 1cm/
   ½-inch pieces

1. Mix the cornflour, salt, soy sauce, water and 5ml/1 tsp of the oil together. Put to one side.

2. Heat the remaining oil in a wok and fry the ginger and lamb for 2-3 minutes.

3. Add the onions, green pepper and curry powder and stir fry for 3-4 minutes.

4. Stir in the cornflour mixture and cook for 1 minute.

5. Add the tomatoes and cook until the sauce thickens. Remove the slice of ginger before serving.

TIME: Preparation takes 20 minutes, cooking takes about 10 minutes.

BUYING GUIDE: Fresh root ginger is now widely available. When buying look for a plump, smooth root.

# SWEET AND SOUR BEEF

*The combination of sweet and sour is an
old favourite for Chinese food lovers.*

*SERVES 2*

*Batter*
100g/4oz plain flour
7.5ml/1½ tsps baking powder
60ml/4 tbsps cornflour
15ml/1 tbsp oil
45ml/3 tbsps oil
225g/8oz fillet of beef, cut into 2.5cm/
    1-inch cubes
1 onion, peeled and cut into wedges
2.5cm/1 inch fresh root ginger, peeled and
    thinly sliced
1 clove garlic, peeled and crushed
1 green pepper, seeded and chopped

*Sweet and Sour Sauce*
60ml/4 tbsps sugar
¼ tsp salt
60ml/4 tbsps red or malt vinegar
5ml/1 tsp fresh root ginger, peeled and
    minced
90ml/6 tbsps water
15ml/1 tbsp cornflour or arrowroot
10ml/2 tsps cooked oil
Few drops food colouring
Oil for deep frying

**1.** For the batter: sieve the flour, baking
powder and cornflour.

**2.** Beat in the 1 tbsp oil and add sufficient
water to make a thick, smooth batter.

**3.** Heat the 45ml/3 tbsps oil in a wok and
stir-fry the beef for 2 minutes. Remove
the beef.

**4.** Fry the onion, ginger, garlic and green
pepper for 2-3 minutes in the same oil.
Remove the wok from the heat.

**5.** Mix the sauce ingredients together and
add to the wok. Return the wok to the
heat and bring to the boil gently. Lower
the heat and simmer gently for 2-3
minutes until thick and clear.

**6.** Meanwhile, dip the beef cubes into the
batter and deep fry in the hot oil until
golden brown and crisp.

**7.** Drain on absorbent paper. Arrange in a
deep dish and pour the hot sauce over the
beef. Serve with a chow mein dish or fried
rice.

TIME: Preparation takes 15 minutes, cooking takes 15 minutes.

VARIATION: Thinly sliced carrots, cucumber and courgette may also be
added along with the onion, ginger and green pepper.

# PORK SPARE RIBS

*A great restaurant favourite which tastes just as good made at home.*

*SERVES 4*

16-20 spare ribs
5g/1 tsp salt
Oil
5ml/1 tsp ginger paste
5ml/1 tsp garlic paste
5ml/1 tsp onion paste
Pinch monosodium glutamate (optional)
5ml/1 tsp light soy sauce
5g/1 tsp cornflour
1 egg
½ tsp Shao Hsing wine or dry sherry
½ tsp chilli oil

*Sauce*
45g/3 tbsps sugar
45ml/3 tbsps black vinegar
15ml/1 tbsp tomato ketchup (optional)
5g/1 tsp cornflour
5ml/1 tsp water
15ml/1 tbsp dark soy sauce
½ tsp salt
½ tsp freshly ground black pepper

1. Trim excess fat from spare ribs and rub with salt. Add 60ml/4 tbsps oil to the wok and fry the ginger, garlic and onion for 1-2 minutes. Add the spare ribs and stir-fry for 6 minutes.

2. Remove to a dish and add the monosodium glutamate, light soy sauce, cornflour, egg, wine and chilli oil. Marinate for 10 minutes.

3. Prepare the sauce by mixing all the sauce ingredients together in the wok and bringing them gently to the boil. Simmer for 2-3 minutes and add the spare ribs along with their marinade. Stir fry until the liquid is reduced to half its original quantity.

4. Put all the ingredients onto a baking tray and spread out evenly. Bake at 190°C/375°F/Gas mark 5, for 25 minutes. Baste occasionally with the liquid from the tray and oil. The spare ribs should have browned well and be well coated with seasoning. Serve hot or cold.

TIME: Preparation takes 25 minutes, cooking takes 40-45 minutes.

BUYING GUIDE: Monosodium glutamate is available in most good supermarkets.

# BEEF WITH BROCCOLI

*The traditional Chinese method of cutting meat for
stir-frying, used in this recipe, ensures that the
meat will be tender and will cook quickly.*

*SERVES 2-3*

450g/1lb rump steak, partially frozen
60ml/4 tbsps dark soy sauce
15g/1 tbsp cornflour
15ml/1 tbp dry sherry
5g/1 tsp sugar
225g/8oz fresh broccoli
2.5cm/1-inch piece ginger, peeled and
    shredded
90ml/6 tbsps oil
Salt and pepper

1. Trim any fat from the meat and cut into
very thin strips across the grain. Strips
should be about 7.5cm/3-inches long.

2. Combine the meat with the soy sauce,
cornflour, sherry and sugar. Stir well and
leave long enough for the meat to
completely defrost.

3. Trim the florets from the stalks of the
broccoli and cut them into even-sized
pieces. Peel the stalks of the broccoli and
cut into thin, diagonal slices.

4. Slice the ginger into shreds. Heat a wok
and add 30ml/2 tbsps of the oil to it. Add
the broccoli and sprinkle with salt and
pepper. Stir-fry, turning constantly, until
the broccoli is dark green. Do not cook
for longer than 2 minutes. Remove from
the wok and set aside.

5. Place the remaining oil in the wok and
add the ginger and beef. Stir-fry, turning
constantly, for about 2 minutes. Return the
broccoli to the pan and mix well. Heat
through for 30 seconds and serve
immediately.

TIME: Preparation takes about 25 minutes and cooking takes about 4 minutes.

PREPARATION: Using meat that is partially frozen makes it easier to get very thin slices.

COOK'S TIP: If more sauce is desired, double the quantities of soy sauce, cornflour, dry
sherry and sugar.

# FILLET STEAK CHINESE STYLE

*Fillet steak is best for this quick-fry recipe.*

*SERVES 4*

225g/8oz fillet or rump steak, cut into 2.5cm/1-inch pieces
Pinch of bicarbonate of soda
15ml/1 tbsp light soy sauce
5g/1 tsp sesame oil
5ml/1 tsp Chinese wine, or 10ml/2 tsps dry sherry
10g/2 tsps sugar
5g/1 tsp cornflour
Salt
Pepper
30ml/2 tbsps dark soy sauce
60ml/4 tbsps water
45ml/2 tbsps peanut oil
2 cloves garlic, crushed
2 spring onions, sliced diagonally into 1.5cm/½-inch pieces
½ tsp crushed ginger
1 can straw mushrooms, drained
1 can baby sweetcorn, drained
15ml/1 tbsp oyster sauce

*Garnish*
Spring onion flowers (cut spring onions into 5cm/2 inch lengths. Carefully cut into fine shreds, keeping one end intact, and then soak in cold water until curling)

1. Put steak in a bowl and sprinkle over bicarbonate of soda.

2. Mix together light soy sauce, sesame oil, wine, half the sugar, half the cornflour, and seasoning. Pour over the steak and leave for at least one hour, turning meat occasionally.

3. Meanwhile, make sauce by mixing 30ml/2 tbsps of dark soy sauce, remaining sugar and cornflour, and water. Mix together and set aside.

4. Heat wok, add peanut oil and, when hot, fry steak for 4 minutes. Remove from wok and set aside.

5. Add garlic, spring onions, ginger, mushrooms, baby sweetcorn, and finally steak.

6. Add oyster sauce and mix well. Add sauce mixture and bring to the boil. Cook for 3 minutes, stirring occasionally.

7. Serve hot with rice, garnished with spring onion flowers.

TIME: Preparation takes 1 hour 15 minutes, cooking takes 20 minutes.

# PORK WITH GREEN PEPPERS

*A quickly-prepared stir-fried pork dish with
green peppers and a Hoisin-based sauce.*

*SERVES 4*

450g/1lb pork fillet
30ml/2 tbsps oil
½ tsp chopped garlic
2 green peppers, seeded and cut into thin
   matchsticks
5ml/1 tsp wine vinegar
30ml/2 tbsps chicken stock
15ml/1 tbsp Hoisin sauce
Salt and pepper
5g/1 tsp cornflour, combined with a little
   water

1. Slice the pork thinly, then cut into
narrow strips. Heat the oil in a wok. Add
the garlic, green pepper and the meat. Stir
together well. Cook for 1 minute, shaking
the wok occasionally.

2. Stir in the vinegar, stock and Hoisin
sauce. Season to taste with salt and
pepper. Cook for 3 minutes.

3. Stir in the cornflour and cook, stirring
continuously, until the desired consistency
is reached.

TIME: Preparation takes about 10 minutes and cooking takes 5 minutes.

VARIATION: Replace the green pepper with a red one.

WATCHPOINT: It is not necessary to add sugar to this sauce, as the
Hoisin sauce is sweet enough.

# FIVE-SPICE BEEF WITH BROCCOLI

*A traditional recipe boosted by the addition of five-spice powder.*

*SERVES 2*

225g/8oz fillet or rump steak
1 clove garlic, crushed
½ tsp finely grated ginger
½ tsp five-spice powder
30ml/2 tbsps peanut oil
100g/4oz broccoli florets
Bunch of chives, snipped into 2.5cm/
    1-inch lengths
½ tsp salt
15ml/1 tbsp dark soy sauce
140ml/¼ pint  hot water
2 tsps cornflour, slaked in 15ml/1 tbsp
    cold water

1. Cut steak into thin slices, then into narrow strips. Mix together with garlic, ginger, and five-spice powder.

2. Heat wok, add 15ml/1 tbsp of oil, and stir-fry broccoli for 8 minutes.

3. Remove broccoli and add remaining oil.

4. Add meat, and stir-fry for 3 minutes.

5. Add broccoli, soy sauce, salt and water, and heat to simmering point.

6. Mix cornflour with cold water, and pour into wok, stirring continuously until liquid thickens.

7. Toss in chives, stir, and serve immediately with boiled rice.

TIME: Preparation takes 15 minutes, cooking takes 15 minutes.

COOK'S TIP: Five-spice is a compound of different spices which accentuate Chinese recipes.

# BEEF WITH ONIONS

*Marinated beef, sautéed with onions, garlic and
ginger and served in a smooth sauce.*

*SERVES 4*

450g/1lb fillet steak

*Marinade*
15ml/1 tbsp oil
5ml/1 tsp sesame oil
15ml/1 tbsp Chinese wine

15ml/1 tbsp oil
1 piece fresh ginger root, peeled and
   roughly chopped
3 onions, finely sliced
1 garlic clove, chopped
280ml/½ pint beef stock
1 pinch of sugar
30ml/2 tbsps dark soy sauce
5g/1 tsp cornflour, combined with a little
   water
Salt and pepper

1. Cut the fillet into very thin slices.

2. Mix together the marinade ingredients
and stir in the meat. Leave to marinate for
30 minutes.

3. Heat 1 tbsp oil in a wok and sauté the
ginger, onions and garlic until lightly
browned.

4. Lift the meat out of the marinade with a
slotted spoon and discard the marinade.
Add the meat to the wok and sauté with
the vegetables.

6. Thicken the sauce with the cornflour,
stirring continuously until the desired
consistency is reached. Season with salt
and pepper and serve immediately.

TIME: Preparation takes about 15 minutes and cooking takes approximately 20 minutes.

SERVING IDEA: Serve this dish on a bed of boiled or steamed white rice.

CHECKPOINT: If you use a wok, watch the cooking process carefully, as the
ingredients cook very quickly.

# Sweet and Sour Pork

*This really needs no introduction because of its popularity.
The dish originated in Canton, but is reproduced
in most of the world's Chinese restaurants.*

*SERVES 2-4*

---

100g/4oz plain flour
60g/4 tbsps cornflour
7.5ml/1½ tsps baking powder
Pinch salt
15ml/1 tbsp oil
Water
225g/8oz pork fillet, cut into 1.25cm/½-inch cubes

1 onion, sliced
1 green pepper, seeded, cored and sliced
1 small can pineapple chunks, juice reserved
Oil for frying

*Sweet and Sour Sauce*
30g/2 tbsps cornflour
100g/4oz light brown sugar
Pinch salt
100ml/4 fl oz cider vinegar or rice vinegar
1 clove garlic, crushed
5g/1 tsp fresh ginger, grated
90ml/6 tbsps tomato ketchup
90ml/6 tbsps reserved pineapple juice

---

1. To prepare the batter, sift the flour, cornflour, baking powder and salt into a bowl. Make a well in the centre and add the oil and enough water to make a thick, smooth batter. Using a wooden spoon, stir the ingredients in the well, gradually incorporating flour from the outside, and beat until smooth.

2. Heat enough oil in a wok to deep-fry the pork. Dip the pork cubes one at a time into the batter and drop into the hot oil. Fry 4-5 pieces of pork at a time and remove them with a draining spoon to paper towels. Continue until all the pork is fried.

3. Pour off most of the oil from the wok and add the sliced onion, pepper and pineapple. Cook over high heat for 1-2 minutes. Remove and set aside.

4. Mix all the sauce ingredients together and pour into the wok. Bring slowly to the boil, stirring continuously until thickened. Allow to simmer for about 1-2 minutes or until completely clear.

5. Add the vegetables, pineapple and pork cubes to the sauce and stir to coat completely. Reheat for 1-2 minutes and serve immediately.

---

TIME: Preparation takes about 15 minutes, cooking takes about 15 minutes.

VARIATION: Use beef or chicken instead of the pork. Uncooked, peeled prawns may be used as can whitefish, cut into 2.5cm/1-inch pieces.

# SPICED BEEF

*A classic recipe which requires the best-quality beef.*

*SERVES 2-3*

*Marinade*
5g/1 tsp sugar
2-3 star anise, ground
½ tsp ground fennel
15ml/1 tbsp dark soy sauce
¼ tsp monosodium glutamate (optional)

450g/1lb fillet of beef, cut into 2.5cm/
   1-inch strips
2.5cm/1 inch fresh root ginger, peeled and
   crushed
½ tsp salt
30ml/2 tbsps oil
4 spring onions, sliced
½ tsp freshly ground black pepper
15ml/1 tbsp light soy sauce

1. Mix the marinade ingredients together.

2. Add the beef strips, ginger and salt, and marinate for 20 minutes.

3. Heat the oil in wok and stir-fry the onions for 1 minute.

4. Add the beef, ground pepper and soy sauce and stir-fry for 4-5 minutes.

TIME: Preparation takes 30 minutes, cooking takes 5-6 minutes.

COOK'S TIP: Fresh root ginger keeps well if wrapped in food wrap and stored in the refrigerator.

# MEAT AND PRAWN CHOW MEIN

*This chow mein is a wonderful mix
of vegetables, meat and seafood.*

*SERVES 4*

450g/1lb dried Chinese noodles or broken
   spaghetti
60ml/4 tbsps oil
2-3 spring onions, chopped
100g/4oz cooked ham, shredded
100g/4oz peeled prawns
100g/4oz shredded carrots
100g/4oz green beans, sliced
Salt to taste
5g/1 tsp sugar
5ml/1 tbsp rice wine or dry sherry
100g/4oz cooked chicken, shredded
100g/4oz bean sprouts
37ml/2½ tbsps soy sauce

**1.** Cook the noodles in boiling, salted water for 4-5 minutes. Rinse under cold water and drain thoroughly.

**2.** Toss in 15ml/1 tbsp oil. Heat the remaining oil in a wok.

**3.** Add the onions, ham, prawns, carrots and green beans and stir-fry for 2-3 minutes.

**4.** Add the salt, sugar, wine, chicken and bean sprouts. Cook for 2 minutes.

**5.** Add the cooked noodles and soy sauce. Cook for 1-2 minutes. Serve immediately.

TIME: Preparation takes 20 minutes, cooking takes 12-15 minutes.

# SWEET AND SOUR PORK AND PINEAPPLE

*Sweet and sour recipes are perfect for mixed
gatherings as children often enjoy them as much as adults.*

*SERVES 4*

450g/1lb lean pork fillet, cut into 2.5cm/
   1-inch cubes
30ml/2 tbsps light soy sauce
30ml/2 tbsps white wine vinegar
30g/2 tbsps tomato purée
15g/1 tbsp sugar
30ml/2 tbsps peanut oil
15g/1 tbsp cornflour
1 clove garlic, crushed
5g/1 tsp grated root ginger
¼ pint water
1 can pineapple pieces, drained
Fresh Chinese parsley (coriander) to garnish

**1.** Place pork in bowl. Pour over light soy sauce and toss together. Leave for 15 minutes.

**2.** Mix together vinegar, tomato purée and sugar, and set aside.

**3.** Heat wok and add oil. Remove pork from soy sauce, and add soy sauce to sauce mixture.

**4.** Toss pork in cornflour, coating well. When oil is hot, brown pork well all over.

**5.** Remove from pan and reduce heat. Fry garlic and ginger for 30 seconds.

**6.** Add water. Bring to the boil, then return pork to wok. Reduce heat; cover and simmer for 15 minutes, stirring occasionally.

**7.** Add sauce mixture and pineapple, and simmer for a further 15 minutes. Garnish with Chinese parsley.

TIME: Preparation takes 20 minutes, cooking takes 45 minutes.

SERVING IDEA: Serve with rice or noodles.

135

# STIR-FRY BEEF WITH MANGO SLICES

*This oriental combination of ingredients is refreshingly different.*

*SERVES 2-3*

225g/½lb fillet of beef
15ml/1 tbsp cooking wine
15ml/1 tbsp soy sauce
5g/1 tsp cornflour
¼ tsp sugar
¼ tsp pepper
1 large mango
60g/4 tbsps oil
15g/1 tbsp shredded ginger root
15g/1 tbsp shredded spring onions

1. Cut beef into thin bite-sized slices. Marinate in the wine, soy sauce, cornflour, sugar and pepper for 20 minutes.

2. Skin mango, cut into ¼-inch thick slices.

3. Set wok over a high heat, pour 4 tbsps oil into the wok, wait until it's almost smoking. Reduce heat to moderate, stir-fry the beef and ginger for 1-2 minutes. Remove with a slotted spoon.

4. Toss the mango slices in the hot oil for a few seconds, return the beef and ginger, and spring onions. Stir over the heat for a further few seconds. Serve immediately.

TIME: Preparation takes 30 minutes, cooking takes about 3 minutes.

COOK'S TIP: If you cannot get a fresh mango – tinned mango is available from supermarkets.

# LAMB MEATBALLS WITH YOGURT

*A refreshing recipe which will have everyone asking for more.*

*SERVES 3-4*

450g/1lb lean minced lamb
2 cloves garlic, crushed
1 small onion, peeled and grated
½ tsp chilli powder
5g/1 tsp garam masala
15g/1 tbsp chopped mint
25g/1oz breadcrumbs
1 egg, lightly beaten
Salt
Pepper
30ml/2 tbsps oil
Small pinch of salmon strands, or ¼ tsp
    ground turmeric
30ml/2 tbsps boiling water
75ml/5 tbsps plain yogurt
Fresh Chinese parsley (coriander) or mint
to garnish

1. In a bowl, mix together minced lamb, garlic, onion, chilli powder, garam masala, mint and breadcrumbs.

2. Add lightly beaten egg to bind ingredients together. Add salt and pepper to taste.

3. Wet hands. Take a teaspoon of mixture, and roll between palms, forming small balls.

4. Heat wok and add oil. Add meatballs, shake wok to make meatballs roll around, and fry until browned well all over.

5. Add saffron or turmeric to 30ml/2 tbsps boiling water. Leave for 5 minutes.

6. Add water to yogurt, and stir in until evenly mixed. Reheat meatballs and serve on yogurt.

7. Garnish with mint or fresh coriander. Serve with rice.

TIME: Preparation takes 15 minutes, cooking takes 30 minutes.

COOK'S TIP: Saffron is expensive, so if you do not intend to use it very often it may be better to use turmeric.

# CARAMELISED SPARERIBS

*These sweet, caramelised spareribs are always a
success. Tell guests to use their fingers; knives
or chopsticks are out of the question.*

*SERVES 4*

1 carrot
1 bay leaf
1 leek
900g/2lbs pork spareribs, separated
5ml/1 tbsp honey
15ml/1 tbsp white wine vinegar
5g/1 tsp chopped garlic
30ml/2 tbsps soy sauce
75ml/3 fl oz chicken stock
Salt and pepper

**1.** In a large saucepan combine 4 cups
water with the carrot, bay leaf and leek.
Bring to the boil and add the spareribs.
Blanch the meat for 10 minutes, remove
from the stock and drain well.

**2.** Lay the ribs in an ovenproof pan.
Combine the honey, vinegar and garlic,
and spread the mixture on the ribs.

**3.** Add the soy sauce and the stock to the
dish. Season well with salt and pepper.

**4.** Put into a very hot oven, 240°C/475°F/
Gas Mark 9, and cook until the ribs are
caramelised and have turned a rich, dark
brown colour.

TIME: Preparation takes about 5 minutes and cooking takes approximately
55 minutes, from start to finish.

SERVING IDEA: Serve on a bed of finely shredded lettuce leaves, lightly
seasoned with salt and pepper.

# BEEF WITH GREEN PEPPER AND CHILLI

*The classic mix of beef and green pepper is
given extra punch by the addition of chilli peppers.*

*SERVES 4*

450g/1lb fillet of beef, cut into 2.5cm/
   1-inch strips
*Seasoning*
30ml/2 tbsps dark soy sauce
5g/1 tsp sesame oil
Pinch bicarbonate of soda
¼ tsp ground black pepper
½ tsp salt

Oil for cooking
2 green peppers, seeded and thinly sliced
1 onion, peeled and sliced
2 spring onions, chopped
2.5cm/1 inch fresh root ginger, peeled and
   sliced
2 garlic cloves, peeled and chopped
3 green chillies, sliced

*Sauce*
30ml/2 tbsps chicken stock
½ tsp monosodium glutamate (optional)
5ml/1 tsp dark soy sauce
Salt to taste
Few drops sesame oil

1. Marinate beef with the seasoning
ingredients for 15 minutes.

2. Heat 30ml/2 tbsps oil and stir-fry green
pepper and onions for 2 minutes. Remove
to a plate.

3. Reheat wok, add 2-3 tbsps oil and fry
ginger, garlic and green chillies for 1
minute.

4. Add beef and stir-fry for 4-5 minutes.
Add sauce ingredients, mixed together,
and the fried peppers and onions. Stir fry
for a further 2 minutes, remove ginger
slice and serve.

TIME: Preparation takes 30 minutes, cooking takes 10-12 minutes.

# BEEF STEAK WITH GINGER

*Fresh root ginger accentuates the beef perfectly in this spicy recipe.*

*SERVES*

*Seasoning*
½ tsp bicarbonate of soda
45ml/3 tbsps light soy sauce
30ml/2 tbsps rice wine or dry sherry
½ tsp salt
½ tsp ground black pepper

½ tsp fresh root ginger, peeled and
  minced
225g/½lb beef fillet, sliced into 2.5cm/
  1-inch pieces

*Sauce*
5g/1 tsp sugar
¼ tsp monosodium glutamate (optional)
15ml/1 tbsp dark soy sauce
45ml/3 tbsps stock
Few drops sesame oil
1 tsp Shao Hsing wine or dry sherry

60ml/4 tbsps oil
2.5cm/1 inch fresh root ginger, peeled and
  thinly sliced
4 spring onions, chopped
50g/2oz bamboo shoots, thinly sliced
2 green chillies, sliced

1. Mix the seasoning ingredients with the minced ginger. Add the beef and marinate for 20 minutes. Drain the beef and discard the marinade.

2. Mix the sauce ingredients together.

3. Heat 45ml/3 tbsps oil in the wok and fry the sliced ginger and onion for 2 minutes.

4. Add the bamboo shoots and chillies and stir-fry for 2 minutes. Remove to a plate.

5. Add the remaining oil to the wok and fry the beef for 2-3 minutes.

6. Add fried vegetables and stir fry for 2 minutes. Add well-stirred sauce ingredients and simmer gently as the mixture thickens. Simmer another 1-2 minutes. Remove from heat and serve.

TIME: Preparation takes 20-25 minutes, cooking takes 10-12 minutes.

144

# PORK MEAT BALLS IN SAUCE

*This delicious dish is well worth the effort.*

*SERVES 4*

*Seasoning*
Pinch monosodium glutamate (optional)
15ml/1 tbsp Shao Hsing wine or dry
    sherry
2.5cm/1-inch fresh root ginger, peeled and
    ground
2 spring onions, white part only, minced
½ tsp salt
10g/2 tsps cornflour

450g/1lb lean pork, minced
25g/1oz bamboo shoots, chopped
50g/2oz dried Chinese mushrooms,
    soaked, drained and sliced
1 egg, beaten
Cornflour to roll the meatballs in
175g/6oz Chinese white cabbage, cut into
    7.5cm/3-inch pieces or 225g/8oz
    ordinary green leafy cabbage, cut into
    7.5cm/3-inch pieces
15ml/1 tbsp cooked oil
Oil for deep frying
15g/1 tbsp cornflour
45ml/3 tbsps water
1 small onion, peeled and finely chopped
2.5cm/1-inch fresh root ginger, peeled and
    finely chopped
280ml/½ pint chicken stock

*Sauce*
Salt to taste
½ tsp monosodium glutamate (optional)
15ml/1 tbsp light soy sauce
5ml/1 tsp dark soy sauce
15ml/1 tbsp cooked oil

1. Mix seasoning ingredients together.

2. Add the pork, bamboo shoot, mushrooms and egg and mix well.

3. Shape into 15-16 even-sized balls and roll them in cornflour. Keep aside on a dish.

4. Blanch cabbage for 1 minute in boiling water and the cooked oil. Drain the cabbage and discard the water.

5. Heat the wok and add the oil for deep frying. When quite hot deep-fry the meat balls, a few at a time for 4-5 minutes. Remove and drain. Keep warm in a large casserole dish.

6. Mix the cornflour with the water and set aside.

7. Reheat the wok and add a teaspoon of oil. Stir-fry the ginger and onion for 2 minutes.

8. Add the chicken stock and stir in the blended sauce ingredients. Bring to the boil and add the meat balls. Simmer gently for 30 minutes.

9. Add the cabbage, sesame oil and the blended cornflour mixture. Stir over the heat until sauce thickens.

TIME: Preparation takes 25 minutes, cooking takes 45 minutes.

BUYING GUIDE: Dried Chinese mushrooms are available in delicatessens and Chinese supermarkets.

# PEKING BEEF

*In China, meat is often simmered in large earthenware
casseroles, but a wok is a convenient subsiitute.*

*SERVES 8*

900g/2lb joint of beef
430ml/¾ pint white wine
570ml/1 pint water
2 whole spring onions, roots trimmed
2.5cm/1-inch piece fresh ginger
3 star anise
10g/2 tsps sugar
140ml/¼ pint soy sauce
1 carrot, peeled
2 sticks celery
½ mooli (daikon) radish, peeled

**1.** Place the beef in a wok and add the
white wine, water, spring onions, ginger
and anise. Cover and simmer for about 1
hour.

**2.** Add the sugar and soy sauce, stir and
simmer for 30 minutes longer, or until the
beef is tender. Allow to cool in the liquid.

**3.** Shred all the vegetables finely. Blanch
them all, except the spring onion, in
boiling water for about 1 minute. Rinse
under cold water, drain and leave to dry.

**4.** When the meat is cold, remove it from
the liquid and cut into thin slices. Arrange
on a serving plate and strain the liquid
over it. Scatter over the shredded
vegetables and serve cold.

TIME: Preparation takes about 25 minutes if shredding the vegetables by hand.
This can also be done with the fine shredding blade of a food processor.
Cooking takes about 1½ hours.

ECONOMY: Because of the long cooking time, less expensive cuts of meat may
be used for this dish.

COOK'S TIP: If using a rolled roast, remove as much of the fat from the outside as
possible. Skim off any fat that rises to the surface of the liquid as it cools, before
pouring over the meat to serve.

# LAMB CURRY

*Lamb absorbs flavours well and is
therefore perfect for curries.*

*SERVES 2-3*

30ml/2 tbsps oil
1 onion, peeled and chopped
2.5cm/1 inch fresh root ginger, peeled and
　chopped
2 cloves of garlic, chopped
450g/1lb lean, boned lamb, cut into cubes
1-2 carrots, scraped and sliced
5g/1 tsp five-spice mixture
Salt to taste
2 chillies, chopped
15ml/1 tbsp tomato purée
10g/2 tsps cornflour
1 green pepper, seeded and chopped

**1.** Heat the oil and fry the onion for 2
minutes. Add the ginger and garlic and fry
for 1 minute.

**2.** Add the lamb and carrots and stir-fry for
3-4 minutes. Sprinkle over the five-spice
powder and add the salt, chillies and
tomato purée.

**3.** Stir in 280ml/½ pint water. Cover and
simmer for 30-35 minutes.

**4.** Mix 30ml/2 tbsps water with the
cornflour and add to the curry.

**5.** Add the green pepper and simmer for 5
minutes. Serve with rice.

TIME: Preparation takes 15 minutes, cooking takes 50 minutes.

BUYING GUIDE: Five-spice is a mixture of some of the most commonly used spices in
Chinese cooking. It is available in good supermarkets and delicatessens.

# SWEET PORK WITH VEGETABLES

*Pork with matchstick vegetables in a marvellous sweet and sour sauce.*

*SERVES 4*

1 onion
¼ cucumber
½ red pepper, seeded
½ green pepper, seeded
1 slice pineapple, fresh or canned
60ml/4 tbsps pineapple juice
45ml/3 tbsps wine vinegar
5g/1 tsp chilli sauce
15g/1 tbsp sugar
½ tomato, peeled, seeded and crushed
340ml/12 fl oz chicken stock
30ml/2 tbsps oil
1 tsp cornflour, mixed with 1 tsp water
450g/1lb pork, cut into thin strips
1 clove garlic, chopped
Salt and pepper

1. Cut the onion, cucumber, red and green pepper and pineapple into thin matchsticks.

2. In a small bowl, mix together the pineapple juice, vinegar, chilli sauce, sugar, crushed tomato and chicken stock.

3. Heat the oil in a wok, stir-fry the pork and the garlic. Once the meat is golden brown, remove with a slotted spoon and set aside.

4. Add all the vegetables and the pineapple to the wok and stir-fry for minutes.

5. Return the pork to the wok with the vegetables and pineapple and pour over the contents of the bowl. Cook for 3-4 minutes, stirring, and shaking the wok from time to time.

6. Thicken the sauce by adding the cornflour gradually, stirring continuously until the desired consistency is reached. Season to taste with salt and pepper.

7. Serve piping hot.

TIME: Preparation takes about 25 minutes and cooking takes approximately 40 minutes.

VARIATION: Replace the pineapple juice with orange juice.

WATCHPOINT: The vegetables must be stir-fried quickly so that they remain slightly crisp.

# BRAISED HONG KONG BEEF

*Cutting the meat into tiny strips reduces the
cooking time of this dish.*

*SERVES 4*

30ml/2 tbsps oil
450g/1lb fillet of beef, sliced into
   matchstick-size strips
1 onion, peeled and sliced
2.5cm/1 inch fresh root ginger, peeled and
   cut into thin strips
3-4 fresh tomatoes, cut into thin wedges
225g/½lb carrots, scraped and cut into
   5cm/2 inch strips
10ml/2 tsps brown sugar
½ tsp five spice powder
30ml/2 tbsps light soy sauce
15ml/1 tbsp rice wine or dry sherry
30ml/2 tbsps water
Salt to taste

1. Heat the oil in a wok and fry the beef for 3-4 minutes. Add the onion, ginger, tomatoes and carrots. Stir fry for 2-3 minutes.

2. Add the sugar, five spice powder, soy sauce, wine and water. Season with salt to taste and cook gently for 8-10 minutes.

TIME: Preparation takes 30 minutes, cooking takes about 15-17 minutes.

BUYING GUIDE: If you cannot get five-spice powder from the supermarket
try a health food shop.

# BEEF WITH GREEN BEANS

*A typically Chinese sauce brings this combination alive.*

*SERVES 2-3*

*Seasoning*
½ tsp bicarbonate of soda
5g/1 tsp cornflour
15ml/1 tbsp light soy sauce
30ml/2 tbsps water
5ml/1 tsp cooked oil
450g/1lb lean beef, thinly sliced into
    2.5cm/1-inch pieces

*Sauce*
¼ tsp salt
5g/1 tsp monosodium glutamate (optional)
5ml/1 tsp light soy sauce
5ml/1 tsp dark soy sauce
5ml/1 tsp Shao Hsing wine or dry sherry
100ml/4 fl oz stock
10g/2 tsps cornflour
45ml/3 tbsps oil

2 cloves of garlic, peeled and sliced
1 onion, peeled and cut into wedges
2.5cm/1 inch fresh ginger root, peeled and
    sliced thinly
175g/6oz Chinese long beans, cut into
    7.5cm/3-inch pieces, or whole tender
    green beans
Salt and freshly ground black pepper to
    taste

1. Mix seasoning ingredients together. Add the beef and marinate for 20 minutes. Drain the meat and discard the marinade.

2. Mix the sauce ingredients together.

3. Heat 30ml/2 tbsps oil in the wok until it smokes. Reduce the heat add the garlic and the beef, and stir-fry for 3-4 minutes. Remove the meat and keep to one side.

4. Add the remaining oil to the wok and add the onion, ginger and long beans and stir-fry for 2-3 minutes. Add fried beef.

5. Cover and fry for a further minute. Stir in the sauce ingredients and bring to the boil. Simmer gently for 2-3 minutes.

6. Season with salt and pepper. Remove from heat and serve.

TIME: Preparation takes 30 minutes, cooking takes 12 minutes.

BUYING GUIDE: Monosodium glutamate should be available from good supermarkets, if not try a delicatessen or health food store.

# DICED PORK WITH WALNUTS

*Walnuts accentuate the pork perfectly in this tasty liaison.*

*SERVES 2*

100g/4oz shelled walnuts
Oil for deep-frying

*Seasoning*
1½ tsp light soy sauce
Few drops sesame oil
Salt and freshly ground black pepper to
    taste
15ml/1 tbsp oil
15ml/1 tbsp water
15g/1 tbsp cornflour
Pinch monosodium glutamate (optional)

225g/½lb pork fillet, cut into cubes
1 carrot, thinly sliced
1 onion, peeled and cut into pieces
3 spring onions, chopped
2.5cm/1 inch fresh root ginger, peeled and
    thinly sliced

*Sauce*
90ml/6 tbsps stock
5g/1 tsp cornflour

1. Cook the walnuts in boiling water for 3-4 minutes. Drain the nuts thoroughly.

2. Deep-fry the walnuts until lightly browned. Remove and drain. Use oil for cooking.

3 Mix the seasoning ingredients together and add the pork. Leave to marinate for 15 minutes. Discard marinade.

4. Heat 30ml/2 tbsps of the walnut oil in the wok and stir-fry the carrots for 2 minutes. Add the onions and root ginger and stir-fry for 1 minute.

5. Add 10m/2 tsps of the sauce stock and remove to a plate. Add the drained pork cubes and 15ml/1 tbsp oil to the wok and stir fry for 4-5 minutes.

6. Mix the remaining stock and the cornflour together for the sauce.

7. Return the walnuts and carrots to the wok, together with the blended sauce ingredients. Mix well and simmer until the sauce thickens.

8. Remove and serve immediately.

TIME: Preparation takes 30 minutes, cooking takes 16-18 minutes.

COOK'S TIP: Monosodium glutamate adds extra strength to the flavour of a dish.

# BEEF WITH TOMATO AND PEPPER IN BLACK BEAN SAUCE

*Black beans are a speciality of Cantonese cooking and give
a pungent, salty taste to stir-fried dishes.*

*SERVES 6*

2 large tomatoes
30g/2 tbsps salted black beans
30ml/2 tbsps water
60ml/4 tbsps dark soy sauce
15g/1 tbsp cornflour
15ml/1 tbsp dry sherry
5g/1 tsp sugar
450g/1lb rump steak, cut into thin strips
1 small green pepper, seeded and cored
60ml/4 tbsps oil
175ml/6 fl oz beef stock
Pinch pepper

1. Core tomatoes and cut them into 16 wedges. Crush the black beans, add the water and set aside.

2. Combine soy sauce, cornflour, sherry, sugar and meat in a bowl and set aside.

3. Cut pepper into 1.25cm/½-inch diagonal pieces. Heat the wok and add the oil. When hot, stir-fry the green pepper pieces for about 1 minute and remove.

4. Add the meat and the soy sauce mixture to the wok and stir-fry for about 2 minutes. Add the soaked black beans and the stock. Bring to the boil and allow to thicken slightly. Return the peppers to the wok and add the tomatoes and pepper. Heat through for 1 minute and serve immediately.

TIME: Preparation takes about 25 minutes, cooking takes about 5 minutes.

SERVING IDEA: Serve with plain boiled rice.

WATCHPOINT: Do not add the tomatoes too early or stir the mixture too vigorously once they are added or they will fall apart easily.

VARIATION: Substitute mange tout for the green peppers in the recipe. Mushrooms may also be added and cooked with the pepper or mange tout.

# STEAMED LAMB WITH MUSHROOM SAUCE

*A great combination that should please most appetites.*

*SERVES 4-6*

1kg/2¼lbs boned leg of lamb, cut
   into strips
2 spring onions, thinly sliced
Salt and freshly ground black pepper
10ml/2 tsps oil
2 cloves of garlic, peeled and sliced
5g/1 tsp cornflour
Pinch monosodium glutamate (optional)
75ml/5 tbsps light soy sauce
45ml/3 tbsps rice wine or dry sherry
1 tsp crushed black pepper
2.5cm/1 inch fresh root ginger, peeled and
   thinly sliced
225g/8oz mushrooms, sliced
Few drops sesame oil

1. Put the lamb into a saucepan and add sufficient water to cover. Boil for 5 minutes. Drain the lamb and retain the water. Arrange the lamb strips in a deep dish and sprinkle the spring onions on top. Season with pepper and salt.

2. Heat the oil in a wok and fry the garlic until brown. Remove the garlic and discard.

3. Mix together the cornflour, monosodium glutamate, soy sauce, wine, crushed pepper, ginger and 60ml/4 tbsps reserved water.

4. Stir the cornflour mixture into the oil in the wok, add the mushrooms and cook for 1-2 minutes. Pour over the lamb.

5. Cover the lamb with overlapping foil and tie around the rim. Put the dish in a steamer and steam over boiling water for 2 hours. Serve with the sesame oil sprinkled over the lamb.

TIME: Preparation takes 20-25 minutes, cooking takes 2 hours 10 minutes.

# PORK WITH BLACK BEAN SAUCE

*A tasty recipe which brings together classic Chinese ingredients.*

*SERVES 2-3*

225g/8oz lean pork, cut into 2.5cm/1-inch cubes
15ml/1 tbsp oil
1 red pepper, cored, seeds removed, and sliced

*Sauce*
3 tbsps black soya beans, rinsed in cold water and crushed with back of a spoon
30ml/2 tbsps Chinese wine, or dry sherry
5g/1 tsp grated ginger
30ml/2 tbsps light soy sauce
3 cloves garlic, crushed
15g/1 tbsp cornflour
140ml/¼ pint water

1. Mix together black beans, wine, ginger, soy sauce and garlic.

2. Blend cornflour with 30ml/2 tbsps of water and add to mixture.

3. Place pork in a bowl, and pour over sauce. Toss together well. Leave for at least 30 minutes.

4. Heat wok, add oil and stir-fry red pepper for 3 minutes. Remove and set aside.

5. Add pork, reserving marinade sauce. Stir-fry pork until browned well all over.

6. Add marinade sauce and remaining water. Bring to the boil. Reduce heat, cover, and gently simmer for about 30 minutes, until pork is tender, stirring occasionally. Add more water if necessary.

7. Just before serving, add red pepper and heat through. Serve with plain white rice.

TIME: Preparation takes 40 minutes, cooking takes 45 minutes.

BUYING GUIDE: Black soya beans are available from health food stores.

# Poultry

Szechuan Chilli Chicken

Chicken Livers with Chinese Leaves
and Almonds

Deep Fried Crispy Chicken

Chicken and Cashew Nuts

Chicken and Bean Sprout Salad

Peking Egg Battered Chicken with Bean
Sprouts, in Onion and Garlic Sauce

Roast Crispy Duck

Chicken with Cloud Ears

Chicken Chop Suey

Chicken Fry with Sauce

Chicken with Walnuts and Celery

Tangerine Peel Chicken

Chicken in Hot Pepper Sauce

Sliced Duck with Bamboo Shoots
and Broccoli

Steamed Chicken

Stewed Chicken and Pineapple

Soy Chicken Wings

Chicken with Bean Sprouts

Chicken and Mushrooms

Duck with Bamboo Shoots

Deep-Fried Chicken with Lemon Slices

# SZECHUAN CHILLI CHICKEN

*If you like chillies this is sure to become a favourite.*

*SERVES 3-4*

340g/¾lb chicken breast meat, cooked
5g/1 tsp salt
1 egg white
75ml/5 tbsps oil
1½ tbsps cornflour
2 slices ginger root
2 small dried chilli peppers
2 green or red peppers
2 fresh chilli peppers
30ml/2 tbsps soy sauce
30ml/2 tbsps wine vinegar

**1.** Cut the chicken into bite-sized pieces. Add the salt, egg white, 1 tbsp oil, and cornflour. Mix and rub these evenly over the chicken pieces to form a thin coating.

**2.** Chop the ginger, and dried chilli. Cut the peppers into bite-sized pieces.

**3.** Heat the remaining oil in a wok. Add the ginger and chilli peppers stir-fry for 1 minute.

**4.** Add the chicken pieces, separating them while stirring. Add the pepper, soy sauce and vinegar; fry for a further 2 minutes.

**5.** Serve immediately with rice.

TIME: Preparation takes 5 minutes, cooking takes 5 minutes.

COOK'S TIP: Vary the amount of chilli peppers according to how hot you like your food!

# CHICKEN LIVERS WITH CHINESE LEAVES AND ALMONDS

*Chicken livers need quick cooking, so they are the perfect choice for the Chinese stir-frying method.*

*SERVES 4*

---

225g/8oz chicken livers
45ml/3 tbsps oil
60g/2oz split blanched almonds
1 clove garlic, peeled
60g/2oz mange tout
8-10 Chinese leaves
10g/2 tsps cornflour mixed with 15ml/
   1 tbsp cold water
30ml/2 tbsps soy sauce
140ml/¼ pint chicken stock

---

1. Pick over the chicken livers and remove any discoloured areas or bits of fat. Cut the chicken livers into even-sized pieces.

2. Heat a wok and pour in the oil. When the oil is hot, turn the head down and add the almonds. Cook, stirring continuously, over gentle heat until the almonds are a nice golden brown. Remove and drain on paper towels.

3. Add the garlic, cook for 1-2 minutes to flavour the oil and remove. Add the chicken livers and cook for about 2-3 minutes, stirring frequently. Remove the chicken livers and set them aside.

4. Add the mange tout to the wok and stir-fry for 1 minute.

5. Shred the Chinese leaves finely, add to the wok and cook for 1 minute. Remove the vegetables and set them aside.

6. Mix together the cornflour and water with the soy sauce and stock. Pour into the wok and bring to the boil. Cook until thickened and clear. Return all the other ingredients to the sauce and reheat for 30 seconds. Serve immediately.

---

TIME: Preparation takes about 25 minutes, cooking takes about 4-5 minutes.

PREPARATION: Remove any discoloured portions from the livers as these can cause a bitter taste. Livers may be served slightly pink in the middle.

SERVING IDEA: Serve with plain or fried rice. Chinese noodles also make a good accompaniment.

# DEEP-FRIED CRISPY CHICKEN

*Everybody loves fried chicken and this recipe is especially tasty.*

*SERVES 4*

1.5kg/3-4lbs chicken, prepared for
  cooking

*Seasoning*
5g/1 tsp salt
½ tsp five-spice powder
40g/1½oz maltose
30ml/2 tbsps malt vinegar
140ml/½ pint white vinegar
Oil for deep frying

**1.** Wash the chicken and hang it up by a hook to drain and dry. The skin will dry quickly. Pour boiling water over the chicken 4-5 times, to partially cook the skin. This will make the skin crisp during frying. Rub salt and five-spice powder well inside the chicken cavity.

**2.** Dissolve the maltose and vinegars in a pan over a gentle heat. Pour over the chicken. Repeat several times, catching the maltose solution in a drip tray.

**3.** Leave the chicken to hang and dry for 1½-2 hours, until the skin is smooth and shiny.

**4.** Heat the oil for deep frying. Deep-fry the chicken for 10 minutes. Ladle hot oil carefully over the chicken continually, until the chicken is deep brown in colour. (The skin puffs out slightly.)

**5.** Cook for a further 3-4 minutes and remove from the oil. Drain on absorbent paper. Cut into small pieces and serve with a dip.

TIME: Preparation takes 3 hours, cooking takes 13-14 minutes.

COOKS TIP: Maltose is similar to molasses and can be substituted by honey, treacle or golden syrup.

# CHICKEN AND CASHEW NUTS

*A popular combination that works extremely well.*

*SERVES 4*

---

350g/12oz chicken breast, sliced into
  2.4cm/1-inch pieces
15g/1 tbsp cornflour

*Seasoning*
5g/1 tsp salt
5ml/1 tsp sesame oil
15ml/1 tbsp light soy sauce
½ tsp sugar

Oil for deep frying
100g/4oz cashew nuts
2 spring onions, chopped
1 small onion, peeled and cubed
2.5cm/1 inch fresh root ginger, peeled and
  sliced
2 cloves of garlic, sliced
75g/3oz mange tout
50g/2oz bamboo shoots, thinly sliced

*Sauce*
10ml/2 tsps cornflour
15ml/1 tbsp Hoisin sauce
200ml (just over ⅓ pint) chicken stock
Pinch monosodium glutamate (optional)

---

1. Roll the chicken pieces in cornflour.
Discard the remaining cornflour.

2. Mix the seasoning ingredients together
and pour over chicken. Leave to stand for
10 minutes.

3. Heat oil for deep frying and fry cashew
nuts until golden brown. Remove the nuts
and drain on kitchen paper.

4. Heat 30ml/2 tbsps oil in a wok and stir-
fry the onions, ginger and garlic for 2-3
minutes.

5. Add mange tout and bamboo shoots
and stir-fry for 3 minutes. Remove the
fried ingredients.

6. Add 15ml/1 tbsp oil to the wok and fry
the chicken for 3-4 minutes. Remove the
chicken.

7. Clean the wok and add a further 10ml/
2 tsps oil and return chicken, cashew nuts
and fried onions etc. to the wok.

8. Prepare the sauce by mixing the
cornflour, Hoisin sauce, chicken stock and
monosodium glutamate together.

9. Pour over the chicken. Mix well and
cook until the sauce thickens and
becomes transparent.

---

TIME: Preparation takes 15 minutes, cooking takes 15 minutes.

VARIATION: A few chunks of pineapple will add extra zest to the dish.

# CHICKEN AND BEAN SPROUT SALAD

*Steamed chicken and bean sprouts, coated in a refreshingly light sauce.*

*SERVES 4*

175g/6oz bean sprouts
340g/12oz chicken breast meat
15ml/1 tbsp soy sauce
30g/2 tbsps chopped chives
15ml/1 tbsp white wine vinegar
5g/1 tsp sugar
5ml/1 tbsp soy sauce
Pinch chopped garlic
15ml/1 tbsp peanut oil
½ tsp sesame oil
Salt and pepper

1. Cook the bean sprouts for 2 minutes in boiling water. Drain and refresh under cold water. Set aside to drain completely.

2. Sprinkle the chicken with 1 tsp soy sauce and cook in a Chinese steamer.

3. Once the chicken is cooked, set it aside to cool and then slice thinly.

4. Prepare the sauce by mixing together the remaining ingredients and seasoning with a little salt and pepper. Allow the sauce to stand for 20 minutes.

5. Mix together the bean sprouts and the chicken. Pour over the sauce and serve.

TIME: Preparation takes about 15 minutes and cooking also takes about 15 minutes.

VARIATION: The chicken could be cooked in stock, to which the soy sauce has been added.

COOK'S TIP: Mix together the sauce ingredients the day before using them. The flavours will have more time to develop fully.

# Peking Egg Battered Chicken with Bean sprouts, in Onion and Garlic Sauce

*This exciting mixture results in a simply delicious dish.*

*SERVES 3*

3 breasts of chicken
Salt and pepper
175g/6oz bean sprouts
2 eggs
2 cloves garlic
2 spring onions
60ml/4 tbsps oil
60ml/4 tbsps stock
Vinegar to taste

**1.** Cut each chicken breast into 4-inch slices. Rub with salt and pepper.

**2.** Beat eggs lightly, and add the chicken slices to the eggs.

**3.** Crush garlic and cut spring onions into 1-inch pieces.

**4.** Heat the oil in the wok. Add the chicken pieces one by one, and reduce heat to low. Leave to sauté for 2-3 minutes.

**5.** Once the egg has set, sprinkle the chicken with garlic and spring onion and bean sprouts.

**6.** Finally, add the stock and vinegar to taste. Simmer gently for 4 minutes.

**7.** Remove the chicken, cut each piece into small regular pieces, serve on a heated platter. Pour the remaining sauce from the pan over the chicken.

TIME: Preparation takes 10 minutes, cooking takes about 10 minutes.

COOK'S TIP: Buy the bean sprouts on the day you intend to use them as they deteriorate rapidly.

# ROAST CRISPY DUCK

*This dish can be served as a main course for 4 or as a starter for 6.*

*SERVES 4-6*

2kg/4½lbs duck or goose, prepared for cooking
60ml/4 tbsps maltose or golden syrup
250ml/8 fl oz water
12 spring onions, cut into 5cm/2-inch lengths
½ tsp red food colouring
30g/2 tbsps tomato purée

*Duck Dip*
100g/4oz sugar
60ml/4 tbsps sweet bean paste
30ml/2 tbsps sesame oil
100ml/4 fl oz water

**1.** Wash the duck and pat it dry on a clean cloth. Ease the finger between the skin and flesh of the duck, starting at the neck end and working the length of the bird. Put a stick or large skewer through the neck and the cavity of the duck to wedge it securely. This will make the duck easier to handle. Hold the duck over the sink and pour boiling water all over it. Pat the duck dry.

**2.** Melt half the maltose and dissolve in the water. Stand the duck on a rack over a deep tray. Slowly pour the maltose liquid over the duck. Pour the maltose liquid over the duck 3 or 4 times. Leave the duck in a cool place for 6-8 hours, or overnight, until the skin is dry.

**3.** Remove the skewer. Stand the duck on a rack in a roasting tin. Preheat the oven to 200°C/400°F/Gas Mark 6 and cook for 30 minutes. Turn over and cook the underside for a further 30 minutes.

**4.** Melt the remaining maltose with the tomato purée and add the food colouring. Spread over the duck and cook for a further 30 minutes. (The duck should have a crisp, red skin.)

**5.** Heat the wok and add the mixed ingredients for the duck dip. Cook for 3-4 minutes until the sugar has dissolved and the dip is smooth. Serve in individual cups.

**6.** Remove the duck skin in squares. Slice the duck flesh and serve with the skin on top.

Time: Preparation takes 15-20 minutes, plus 6-8 hours to dry, cooking takes 1 hour 30 minutes.

181

# CHICKEN WITH CLOUD EARS

*Cloud ears is the delightful name for an edible
tree fungus which is mushroom-like in taste and texture.*

*SERVES 6*

12 cloud ears, wood ears or other dried
  Chinese mushrooms, soaked in boiling
  water for 5 minutes
450g/1lb chicken breasts, boned and
  thinly sliced
1 egg white
10g/2 tsps cornflour
10ml/2 tsps white wine
10ml/2 tsps sesame oil
2.5cm/1-inch piece fresh ginger, left whole
1 clove garlic
280ml/½ pint oil
280ml/½ pint chicken stock
15g/1 tbsp cornflour
45ml/3 tbsps light soy sauce
Pinch salt and pepper

1. Soak the mushrooms until they soften
and swell. Remove all the skin and bone
from the chicken and cut it into thin slices.
Mix the chicken with the egg white,
cornflour, wine and sesame oil.

2. Heat the wok for a few minutes and
pour in the oil. Add the whole piece of
ginger and whole garlic clove to the oil
and cook for about 1 minute. Take them
out and reduce the heat.

3. Add about a quarter of the chicken at a
time and stir-fry for about 1 minute.
Remove and continue cooking until all the
chicken is fried. Remove all but about
30ml/2 tbsps of the oil from the wok.

4. Drain the mushrooms and squeeze
them to extract all the liquid, if using
mushrooms with stems, remove the stems
before slicing thinly. Cut cloud ears or
wood ears into smaller pieces. Add to the
wok and cook for about 1 minute. Add
the stock and allow it to come almost to
the oil. Mix together the cornflour and soy
sauce and add a spoonful of the hot stock.

5. Add the mixture to the wok, stirring
constantly, and bring to the boil. Allow to
boil 1-2 minutes or until thickened. The
sauce will clear when the cornflour has
cooked sufficiently.

6. Return the chicken to the wok and add
salt and pepper. Stir thoroughly for about
1 minute and serve immediately.

TIME: Preparation takes about 25 minutes, cooking takes about 5 minutes.

PREPARATION: If desired, the chicken may be cut into 2.5cm/1-inch cubes. If slicing, cut
across the grain as this helps the chicken to cook more evenly.

BUYING GUIDE: Cloud ears or wood ears are a type of edible Chinese tree fungus. They
are both available from Chinese supermarkets and some delicatessens. Chinese mushrooms
are more readily available from Chinese supermarkets and some delicatessens. Chinese
ingredients are becoming more readily available. Check supermarket shelves for bottled
sauces like Oyster Sauce.

# CHICKEN CHOP SUEY

*Give up the Chinese take-away and create your
own delicious version of this great favourite.*

*SERVES 2-3*

30ml/2 tbsps light soy sauce
1 tsp brown sugar
Salt to taste
450g/1lb boned chicken, cut into 2.5cm/
   1-inch pieces
30ml/2 tbsps cooking oil
1 onion, cut into chunks
225g/8oz bean sprouts
10ml/2 tsps sesame oil
¼ tsp monosodium glutamate (optional)
15g/1 tbsp cornflour
225g/8 fl oz chicken stock

1. Mix the soy sauce with the sugar and
salt and add the chicken pieces. Allow to
marinate for 5 minutes. Drain the chicken
and reserve the marinade.

2. Heat the wok and add the oil. Fry the
chicken for 2-3 minutes. Remove the
chicken.

3. Fry the onions for 2-3 minutes and add
the bean sprouts. Stir-fry for 4-5 minutes.

4. Return the chicken to the pan and add
the sesame oil.

5. Dissolve the monosodium glutamate
and the cornflour in the stock and pour
over the chicken mixture. Cook for 2-3
minutes, stirring, until the sauce thickens.

TIME: Preparation takes 30 minutes, cooking takes 15 minutes.

COOK'S TIP: Bean sprouts should always be bought on the day they are to be
used as they deteriorate rapidly.

# CHICKEN FRY WITH SAUCE

*This recipe is perfect for using the less
popular parts of chicken, such as thighs.*

*SERVES 2*

15ml/1 tbsp cooked oil
5ml/1 tsp sesame oil
25g/1oz sesame seeds

*Sauce*
2 cloves of garlic, minced
2 spring onions, finely chopped or minced
5ml/1 tsp Chinese black vinegar or brown
  malt vinegar
45ml/3 tbsps dark soy sauce
5ml/1 tsp light soy sauce
½ tsp monosodium glutamate (optional)
½ tsp salt
1½ tsps sugar

8 chicken thighs, or 450g/1lb chicken, cut
  into small joints

1. Heat the wok and add the oils. Stir-fry the sesame seeds till they change colour to golden brown. Remove onto a dish.

2. Mix sauce ingredients together and add the sesame seeds.

3. Wipe the wok and add the chicken. Add sufficient water to cover, and cook for 20 minutes until the chicken is tender.

4. De-bone the chicken and quickly cut meat into bite-size pieces.

5. Arrange the chicken on a plate and spoon the sauce over the top. Serve immediately.

TIME: Preparation takes 20 minutes, cooking takes about 24 minutes.

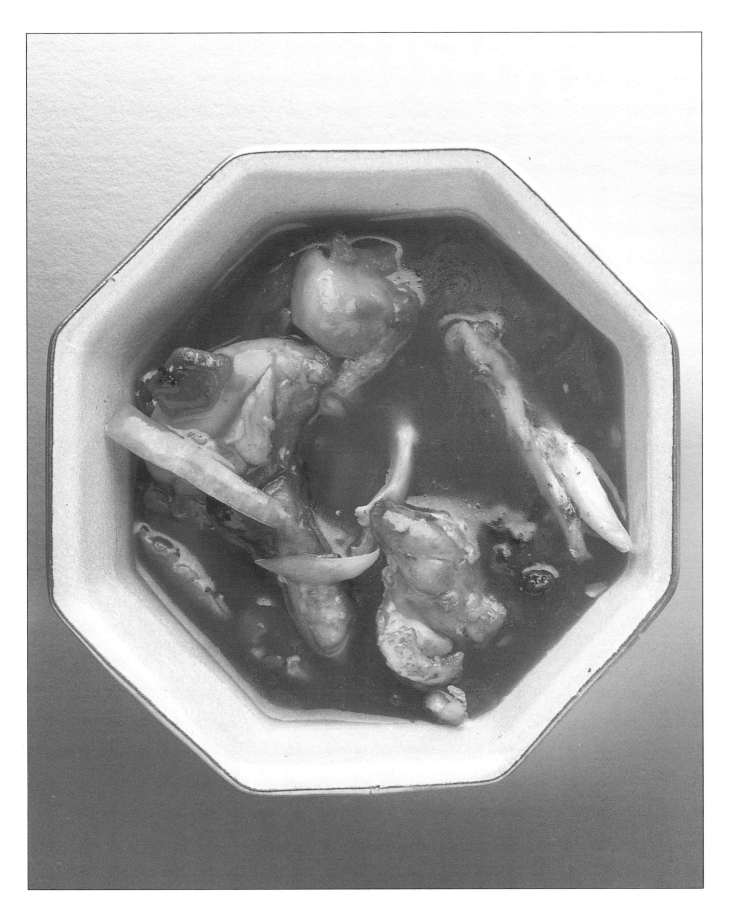

# CHICKEN WITH WALNUTS AND CELERY

*Oyster sauce lends a subtle, slightly salty taste to this Cantonese dish.*

*SERVES 4*

225g/8oz boned chicken, cut into 2.5cm/
   1-inch pieces
10ml/2 tsps soy sauce
10ml/2 tsps brandy
5g/1 tsp cornflour
Salt and pepper
30ml/2 tbsps oil
1 clove garlic, peeled and crushed
100g/4oz walnut halves
3 sticks celery, cut in diagonal slices
140ml/¼ pint water or chicken stock
10ml/2 tsps oyster sauce

1. Combine the chicken with the soy sauce, brandy, cornflour, salt and pepper.

2. Heat a wok and add the oil and garlic. Cook for about 1 minute to flavour the oil.

3. Remove the garlic and add the chicken in two batches. Stir-fry quickly without allowing the chicken to brown. Remove the chicken and add the walnuts to the wok. Cook for about 2 minutes until the walnuts are slightly brown and crisp.

4. Slice the celery, add to the wok and cook for about 1 minute. Add the oyster sauce and water and bring to the boil. When boiling, return the chicken to the pan and stir to coat all the ingredients well. Serve immediately.

TIME: Preparation takes 5 minutes, cooking takes about 15 minutes.

# TANGERINE PEEL CHICKEN

*An exotic mixture of flavours blend perfectly
in this delicious chicken dish.*

*SERVES 2*

450g/1lb boned chicken breast, cut into
    2.5cm/1-inch pieces

*Seasoning*
½ tsp salt
7.5ml/1½ tsps sugar
½ tsp monosodium glutamate (optional)
5ml/1 tsp dark soy sauce
10ml/2 tsps light soy sauce
5ml/1 tsp rice wine or dry sherry
10ml/2 tsps malt vinegar
5ml/1 tsp sesame oil
10g/2 tsps cornflour

Oil for deep frying
1-2 red or green chillies, chopped
1.25cm/½ inch fresh root ginger, peeled
    and finely chopped
5cm/2 inches dried tangerine peel,
    coarsely ground or crumbled
2 spring onions, finely chopped

*Sauce*
½ tsp cornflour
15-30ml/1-2 tbsps water or stock

1. Mix the chicken pieces with the seasoning ingredients and stir well. Leave to marinate for 10-15 minutes. Remove the chicken pieces and reserve the marinade.

2. Heat wok and add the oil for deep frying. Once it starts to smoke add the chicken pieces and fry for 4-5 minutes until golden. Drain chicken on kitchen paper.

3. Pour off the oil, leaving 15ml/1 tbsp oil in the wok, and stir-fry the chillies, ginger, tangerine peel and onions for 2-3 minutes. When they begin to colour add the chicken and stir-fry for 1 minute.

4. Mix the reserved marinade with the sauce ingredients and pour over the chicken. Stir and cook for 2-3 minutes until the sauce thickens and the chicken is tender. Serve immediately.

TIME: Preparation takes 30 minutes, cooking takes 12-15 minutes.

# CHICKEN IN HOT PEPPER SAUCE

*Stir-fried chicken served with peppers in a hot sauce.*

*SERVES 4*

1 chicken
30ml/2 tbsps oil
5g/1 tsp chopped garlic
1 green pepper, seeded and cut into thin
    strips
1 red pepper, seeded and cut into thin
    strips
5ml/1 tsp wine vinegar
15ml/1 tbsp light soy sauce
5g/1 tsp sugar
340ml/12 fl oz chicken stock
15ml/1 tbsp chilli sauce
Salt and pepper

**1.** First, bone the chicken. To bone the legs, cut down along the bone on all sides, drawing out the bone with an even movement. Cut all the chicken meat into thin strips.

**2.** Heat the oil in a wok and stir-fry the garlic, chicken and the green and red peppers.

**3.** Pour off any excess oil and deglaze the wok with the vinegar. Stir in the soy sauce, sugar and stock.

**4.** Gradually stir in the chilli sauce, tasting after each addition. Season with a little salt and pepper to taste.

**5.** Cook until the sauce has reduced slightly. Serve piping hot.

TIME: Preparation takes 10 minutes and cooking takes approximately 25 minutes.

# Sliced Duck with Bamboo Shoots and Broccoli

*A delightful recipe which mixes some of
China's best-loved ingredients.*

*SERVES 2*

1kg/2¼lbs small duck
5g/1 tsp monosodium glutamate (optional)
12.5ml/2½ tsps cornflour
30ml/2 tbsps water
100g/4oz broccoli, chopped
45ml/3 tbsps oil
2-3 spring onions, chopped
2.5cm/1 inch fresh root ginger, peeled and
　　thinly sliced
1 clove garlic, peeled and finely chopped
100g/4oz bamboo shoots, sliced
½ tsp sugar
Salt and freshly ground black pepper to
　　taste
60ml/4 tbsps chicken stock
10ml/2 tsps rice wine or sweet sherry
Few drops sesame oil

1. Cut the duck flesh into bite-size pieces,
removing all the bones.

2. Mix the the monosodium glutamate,
7.5ml/1½tsps cornflour and 1 tbsp water
together. Stir into the duck. Marinate for
20 minutes.

3. Cook the broccoli in boiling water for 1
minute. Drain thoroughly.

4. Heat the wok and add the oil. Stir-fry
the onions, ginger, garlic and bamboo
shoots for 1-2 minutes.

5. Add the duck pieces and stir-fry for 2-3
minutes. Add the sugar, salt and pepper to
taste, stock, rice wine, sesame oil and
broccoli. Stir-fry for 3 minutes.

6. Add the remaining cornflour and water
blended together. Stir over the heat until
the sauce thickens. Serve immediately.

COOK'S TIP: Fresh root ginger keeps well if tightly wrapped in
plastic wrap and stored in the refrigerator.

# STEAMED CHICKEN

*A great method of cooking chicken and
one which brings out all its flavour.*

*SERVES 3-4*

---

750g/1½lbs boned chicken

*Seasoning*
15ml/1 tbsp light soy sauce
5g/1 tsp brown sugar
5g/1 tsp salt
15g/1 tbsp cornflour
30ml/2 tbsps oil or cooked oil
½ tsp monosodium glutamate (optional)

100g/4oz dried mushrooms, soaked in
  boiling water for 5 minutes and sliced,
  or ordinary mushrooms
1cm/½ inch fresh root ginger, peeled and
  sliced
4 spring onions, finely chopped
30ml/2 tbsps stock or water, if needed

1. Cut the chicken into 2.5cm/1-inch pieces. Mix the seasoning ingredients together and mix with the chicken. Leave to marinate for 15 minutes.

2. Place a plate in a steamer and put the chicken, mushrooms, ginger, half the onion and the stock on top. Steam over boiling water for 15-20 minutes.

3. Serve with the remaining onions sprinkled over the chicken. The steaming can also be done on a greased lotus leaf or a banana leaf. The flavour is quite stunning.

---

TIME: Preparation takes 20-30 minutes, cooking takes 15-20 minutes.

COOK'S TIP: If you can obtain dried mushrooms do use them as their flavour is far superior to ordinary mushrooms.

# STEWED CHICKEN AND PINEAPPLE

*Pineapple complements the chicken wonderfully in this dish.*

*SERVES 2-3*

*Seasoning*
30ml/2 tbsps light soy sauce
15ml/1 tbsp oil
15g/1 tbsp cornflour
5g/1 tsp salt
½ tsp sesame oil
30ml/2 tbsps water

750g/1½lbs boned chicken breast, cut
　into cubes

*Sauce*
7.5ml/1½ tsps cornflour
250ml/8 fl oz water or chicken stock
10ml/2 tsps dark soy sauce
Salt to taste

30ml/2 tbsps oil
1 onion, peeled and cut into chunks
2 spring onions, finely chopped
2.5cm/1 inch fresh root ginger, peeled and
　thinly sliced
4-5 pineapple rings, cut into chunks

**1.** Mix the seasoning ingredients together.

**2.** Add the cubed chicken and marinate for 10-12 minutes.

**3.** Mix the sauce ingredients together together in a bowl.

**4.** Heat the oil in a wok and fry the onions for 2 minutes until just tender. Add the drained chicken and fry for 3-4 minutes.

**5.** Add the root ginger and fry for 1 minute.

**6.** Add any remaining marinade and the sauce ingredients and bring to the boil. Cook, stirring until the sauce thickens, then add the pineapple chunks. Heat through. Remove from the heat and serve with fried rice.

TIME: Preparation takes 30 minutes, cooking takes 15 minutes.

198

# Soy Chicken Wings

*These delicious chicken wings can be served on any occasion.*

*SERVES 4*

1kg/2lbs chicken wings
½ tsp crushed root ginger
15ml/1 tbsp light soy sauce
15ml/1 tbsp sugar
5g/1 tsp cornflour
10ml/2 tsps sesame oil
15ml/1 tbsp Chinese wine, or 30ml/
   2 tbsps dry sherry
Salt
Pepper
30ml/2 tbsps peanut oil
2 spring onions, sliced
15ml/1 tbsp dark soy sauce
1 star anise
45ml/3 tbsps water

1. Wash chicken wings and dry on absorbent paper.

2. Mix together ginger, light soy sauce, sugar, cornflour, sesame oil, wine, and seasoning. Pour marinade over chicken wings and leave for at least 1 hour, turning occasionally.

3. Heat peanut oil until very hot. Add spring onions and chicken wings, and fry until chicken is browned well on all sides.

4. Add dark soy sauce, star anise and water. Bring to the boil, and simmer for 15 minutes.

5. Remove star anise. Serve hot or cold.

TIME: Preparation takes 1 hour 10 minutes, cooking takes 20 minutes.

BUYING GUIDE: Peanut oil and sesame oil should both be available from supermarkets.

# CHICKEN WITH BEAN SPROUTS

*Marinated chicken, stir-fried with bean sprouts*
*and served with a sauce based on the marinade.*

*SERVES 4*

1 chicken, boned
15ml/1 tbsp Chinese wine
5g/1 tsp cornflour
100g/4oz bean sprouts
30ml/2 tbsps oil
½ spring onion, finely sliced
5g/1 tsp sugar
280ml/½ pint chicken stock
Salt and pepper

**1.** Bone the chicken and cut the meat into thin slices or strips.

**2.** Place the chicken on a plate and pour over the Chinese wine.

**3.** Sprinkle over the cornflour and stir together well. Leave to marinate for 30 minutes.

**4.** Blanch the bean sprouts in boiling, lightly salted water for 1 minute. Rinse under cold running water and set aside to drain.

**5.** Remove the chicken from the marinade with a spoon. Heat the oil in a wok and stir-fry the onions and the chicken.

**6.** Add the drained bean sprouts and the sugar. Stir in the marinade and the stock. Allow the chicken to cook through, which will take approximately 20 minutes. Check the seasoning adding salt and pepper to taste. Serve immediately.

TIME: Preparation takes about 20 minutes, marinating takes 30 minutes and cooking takes approximately 30 minutes.

VARIATION: Use an ordinary onion if spring onions are not available.

WATCHPOINT: As soon as you add the marinade to the wok, the mixture will thicken so have the stock ready to pour in immediately and stir continuously until all the ingredients have been fully incorporated.

# CHICKEN AND MUSHROOMS

*A classic combination which always tastes great.*

*SERVES 2*

*Seasoning*
½ tsp salt
30ml/2 tbsps light soy sauce
10g/2 tsps cornflour
5ml/1 tsp rice wine or dry sherry
Pinch monosodium glutamate (optional)

225g/½lb chicken breast, cut into bite-
　size pieces

*Sauce*
Salt to taste
Freshly ground black pepper to taste
15ml/1 tbsp light soy sauce
225ml/8 fl oz chicken stock
10g/2 tsps cornflour or arrowroot
5ml/1 tsp oyster sauce

30ml/2 tbsps oil
1 onion, peeled and chopped
1 clove of garlic, sliced
1cm/½ inch fresh root ginger, peeled and
　thinly sliced
3 dried black mushrooms, soaked and
　sliced
50g/2oz open mushrooms, sliced
50g/2oz button mushrooms, sliced

1. Mix the seasoning ingredients together. Marinate the chicken in the seasoning mixture for 10 minutes.

2. Mix the sauce ingredients together.

3. Heat the oil in a wok and fry the onion, garlic and ginger for 2-3 minutes. Remove and put to one side.

4. Fry the drained chicken in the remaining oil for 4 minutes.

5. Add the mushrooms and stir-fry for 1 minute. Add a little extra oil if necessary.

6. Return the fried onion mixture to the wok and stir-fry until well mixed. Pour the blended sauce ingredients into the wok and cook gently until the sauce thickens. Serve piping hot.

TIME: Preparation takes 15 minutes, plus 10 minutes to marinate. Cooking takes 10-12 minutes.

COOK'S TIP: Supermarkets now have a wider range of mushrooms so choose your favourites if you cannot get those in the recipe.

# DUCK WITH BAMBOO SHOOTS

*Stir-fried bamboo shoots, served with duck breasts and Hoisin-based sauce.*

*SERVES 4*

---

100g/4oz bamboo shoots, cut into thin
　slices
50g/2oz sugar
90ml/3 fl oz water
1 tsp chopped fresh ginger root
15ml/1 tbsp Hoisin sauce
2 duck breasts
15ml/1 tbsp oil
Salt and pepper

---

**1.** Cook the bamboo shoots in boiling, lightly salted water for approximately 15 minutes. Drain thoroughly and set aside.

**2.** Mix the sugar and water together in a small saucepan, stirring thoroughly.

**3.** Add the ginger and the Hoisin sauce. Place over a gentle heat and cook until a light syrup is formed.

**4.** Brush this syrup over the duck breasts.

**5.** Heat the oil in a frying pan and add the duck breasts, skin-side down first. Sear on each side. Take out and finish cooking a hot oven, 220°C/425°F/Gas Mark 7 for approximately 15 minutes.

**6.** Shortly before the duck breasts are cooked, stir-fry the bamboo shoots in the oil used to sear the duck breasts. Season with salt and pepper and serve hot with the sliced duck breasts.

---

TIME: Preparation takes about 10 minutes and total cooking time is approximately 50 minutes.

SERVING IDEA: Serve any leftover sauce in a small bowl to accompany the duck.

WATCHPOINT: Don't forget to begin searing the meat in the frying pan skin-side down and then finish with the other side.

# DEEP-FRIED CHICKEN WITH LEMON SLICES

*Lemon complements chicken perfectly in this quick dish.*

*SERVES 6-8*

3lb chicken breast meat
a) ½ tsp salt
   ½ tbsp cooking oil
   ½ tbsp light soy sauce
   15g/1 tbsp cornflour
   15ml/1 tbsp water
   1 egg yolk
   Black pepper
b) 90g/6 tbsps cornflour
   45g/3 tbsps plain flour
c) 45g/3 tbsps sugar
   45ml/3 tbsps lemon juice
   90ml/6 tbsps light broth
   ½ tsp salt
   30g/2 tbsps cornflour
   5ml/1 tsp sesame oil
1 green pepper, cored and seeded
1 red pepper, cored and seeded
Oil for deep frying
2 lemons thinly sliced
Chopped parsley

**1.** Skin the chicken. Cut into bite-sized, thin slices. Marinate chicken in a) for 10 minutes.

**2.** Mix b) on a plate and coat each chicken piece with the mixture.

**3.** Mix c) in a small bowl. Cut pepper into 1-inch pieces.

**4.** Place a 12-inch wok over a high heat. Heat the oil until almost smoking. Deep fry the chicken slices until golden brown.

**5.** Remove with a slotted spoon to a heated plate. Pour off all but a tablespoon of oil.

**6.** Stir-fry the pepper until it begins to brown. Pour in c). Bring to the boil, stirring until thickened.

**7.** Add the chicken pieces. Stir for a further few minutes. Transfer to a heated serving platter, and garnish with lemon slices and chopped parsley.

TIME: Preparation takes 20 minutes, cooking takes about 15 minutes.

# Side Dishes

Bamboo Shoots with Green Vegetables
Stir-fried Rice with Peppers
Fried Vegetables with Ginger
Plain Fried Rice
Szechuan Aubergine
Stir-Fried Chinese Cabbage
Fried Rice
Vegetable Stir-fry
Special Mixed Vegetables
Sweet and Sour Cabbage
Aubergines and Peppers Szechuan Style
Stir-Fried Sticky Rice

# BAMBOO SHOOTS WITH GREEN VEGETABLES

*This side dish is perfect with Peking duck.*

*SERVES 2*

---

Oil for cooking
225g/8oz chopped spinach, or chopped
  broccoli

*Seasoning*
100ml/4 fl oz chicken stock or water
¼ tsp monosodium glutamate (optional)
¼ tsp salt
¼ tsp sugar
100g/4oz bamboo shoots, sliced

*Sauce*
5ml/1 tsp light soy sauce
Pinch monosodium glutamate
5g/1 tsp cornflour
10ml/2 tsps water
15ml/1 tbsp cooked oil

1. Heat 30ml/2 tbsps oil in the wok.

2. Fry the spinach for 2 minutes and add the mixed seasoning ingredients, except the bamboo shoots. Simmer for 1 minute and remove from the wok onto a dish.

3. Heat the wok and add 15ml/1 tbsp oil. Add the bamboo shoots and fry for 1-2 minutes.

4. Return the spinach mixture to the wok. Cook for 30 minutes.

5. Mix together the ingredients for the sauce. Add to the wok and cook for 1-2 minutes.

---

TIME: Preparation takes 10 minutes, cooking takes 10-12 minutes.

COOK'S TIP: Bamboo shoots should always be bought on the day they are to be used as they deteriorate rapidly.

# STIR-FRIED RICE WITH PEPPERS

*Long grain rice stir-fried with red and
green peppers, onions and soy sauce.*

*SERVES 4*

175g/6oz long grain rice
15ml/1 tbsp peanut oil
1 onion, chopped
1 green pepper, seeded and cut into small
　pieces
1 red pepper, seeded and cut into small
　pieces
15ml/1 tbsp soy sauce
Salt and pepper
5ml/1 tsp sesame oil

1. Cook the rice in boiling water, drain
and set aside.

2. Heat the oil in a wok and stir-fry the
onion, add the peppers and fry until
lightly browned.

3. Add the rice to the wok, stir in the soy
sauce and continue cooking until the rice
is heated through completely.

4. Season with salt, pepper and the
sesame oil, and serve.

TIME: Preparation takes 5 minutes and cooking takes approximately 25 minutes.

VARIATION: If you like the strong flavour of sesame oil, stir-fry the vegetables and rice in
this instead of the peanut oil.

Watchpoint: Do not overcook the rice in Step 1, or it will become sticky in Step 3.

# FRIED VEGETABLES WITH GINGER

*Use your imagination with this recipe and adapt it
to whatever greens you can buy.*

*SERVES 4-6*

1kg/2¼lbs mixed Chinese green
   vegetables (cabbage, spinach, kale,
   broccoli, Chinese leaf etc.)
50g/2oz mange tout
5g/1 tsp bicarbonate of soda
10g/2 tsps sugar
5g/1 tsp salt
30ml/2 tbsps oil
2.5cm/1 inch fresh root ginger, peeled and
   shredded
1 green pepper, seeded and diced
1 green or red chilli, sliced into strips

*Sauce*
10ml/2 tsps dark soy sauce
5g/1 tsp sugar
225ml/8 fl oz chicken stock
10g/2 tsps cornflour
5g/1 tsp five spice powder

*To Serve*
2.5ml/½ tsp sesame oil
Freshly ground black pepper to taste

1. Cut greens into 7.5cm/3-inch pieces.
Bring a large pan of water to the boil and
add the sugar and salt.

2. Add the mange tout and greens and
cook for 4-5 minutes. Drain green
vegetables and discard water.

3. Add 15ml/1 tbsp oil to the vegetables
and keep covered. Heat the remaining oil
in the wok and stir fry the ginger for 1
minute.

4. Add the green pepper and chillies and
stir fry for 10-12 minutes. Add the blended
sauce ingredients and stir well. Simmer
gently for 3-4 minutes.

5. Add the green vegetables and cook for
1 minute. Serve immediately, sprinkled
with sesame oil and pepper.

TIME: Preparation takes 10 minutes, cooking takes 13-15 minutes.

# PLAIN FRIED RICE

*Producing perfect rice is a must
for lovers of Chinese food.*

*SERVES*

450g/1lb Patna or long grain rice
¼ tsp monosodium glutamate
30ml/2 tbsps oil
Salt

1. Wash the rice in 4-5 changes of cold water. Drain the rice and put into a large pan or wok. Add sufficient cold water to come 2.5cm/1-inch above the level of the rice. Bring to the boil.

2. Stir once and reduce the heat to simmer. Cover and cook gently for 5-7 minutes until the water has been totally absorbed and the rice is separate and fluffy, with the necessary amount of stickiness to be handled by chopsticks.

3. Spread the rice out on a tray to cool. Sprinkle with the monosodium glutamate. Heat the oil in wok or large frying pan and add the rice. Stir fry for 1-2 minutes.

4. Add salt to taste and stir-fry for a further 1-2 minutes.

TIME: Preparation takes 5 minutes, plus cooling time, cooking takes 10-11 minutes.

# SZECHUAN AUBERGINE

*An unusual side-dish which adds extra spice to meals.*

*SERVES 2*

Oil

1 large European aubergine cut into 5cm/
   2-inch long and 1cm/½ inch thick strips

3 cloves garlic, peeled and finely sliced

2.5cm/1 inch fresh root ginger, peeled and
   shredded

1 onion, peeled and finely chopped

2 spring onions, chopped

100g/4oz cooked and shredded chicken

1 red or green chilli, cut into strips

*Seasoning*

100ml/4 fl oz chicken stock

5g/1 tsp sugar

5ml/1 tsp red vinegar or wine vinegar

½ tsp salt

½ tsp freshly ground black pepper

*Sauce*

5g/1 tsp cornflour

15ml/1 tbsp water

5ml/1 tsp sesame oil

**1.** Heat the wok and add 45ml/3 tbsps oil. Add aubergine and stir fry for 4-5 minutes. The aubergine will absorb a lot of oil; keep stirring or else they will burn. Remove from wok and put to one side.

**2.** Heat the wok and add 30ml/2 tbsps oil. Add the garlic and ginger and fry for 1 minute.

**3.** Add the onions and fry for 2 minutes. Add the chicken and chilli. Cook for 1 minute.

**4.** Return the aubergines to the wok. Add the blended seasoning ingredients and simmer for 6-7 minutes.

**5.** Stir in the blended sauce ingredients and simmer until the sauce thickens. Serve with extra sesame oil if desired.

TIME: Preparation takes 15 minutes, cooking takes 18-20 minutes.

COOK'S TIP: Vary the spiciness of this dish by increasing the quantity of chillies.

# STIR-FRIED CHINESE CABBAGE

*Stir-fried Chinese cabbage, courgettes and pepper,*
*flavoured with sesame oil and soy sauce.*

*SERVES 4*

1 head Chinese cabbage
2 courgettes
30ml/2 tbsps oil
5g/1 tsp chopped garlic
15g/1 tbsp chopped red pepper
15ml/1 tbsp soy sauce
Salt and pepper
Few drops sesame oil

**1.** Shred the Chinese cabbage quite finely.

**2.** Prepare the courgettes, first topping and tailing them and then slicing down the sides, preserving a bit of the flesh with the peel. Slice finely.

**3.** Heat the oil in a wok, add the Chinese cabbage and garlic and stir-fry for 2 minutes.

**4.** Add the courgettes, hot red pepper, soy sauce, salt and pepper. Continue cooking for 3 minutes and serve hot with the sesame oil drizzled on top.

TIME: Preparation takes about 10 minutes and cooking takes approximately 5 minutes.

VARIATION: If you like hot, spicy dishes, add ¼ tsp chilli sauce to the Chinese cabbage.

SERVING IDEA: Cooked in this way, the Chinese cabbage will remain crisp.
If you prefer, cook longer for a softer texture.

# FRIED RICE

*A basic recipe for a traditional Chinese accompaniment to
stir-fried dishes, this can be more substantial with the
addition of meat, poultry or seafood.*

*SERVES 6-8*

450g/1lb cooked rice, well drained and
   dried
45ml/3 tbsps oil
1 egg, beaten
15ml/1 tbsp soy sauce
60g/2oz cooked peas
Dash sesame oil
Salt and pepper
2 spring onions, thinly sliced

**1.** Heat a wok and add the oil. Pour in the
egg and soy sauce and cook until just
beginning to set.

**2.** Add the rice and peas and stir to coat
with the egg mixture. Allow to cook for
about 3 minutes, stirring continuously.
Add seasoning and sesame oil.

**3.** Spoon into a serving dish and sprinkle
over the spring onions.

TIME: The rice will take about 10 minutes to cook. Allow at least 20 minutes for it to drain
as dry as possible. The fried rice dish will take about 4 minutes to cook.

VARIATION: Cooked meat, poultry or seafood may be added to the rice along with the peas.

COOK'S TIP: The 450g/1lb rice measurement is the cooked weight.

224

# VEGETABLE STIR-FRY

*A marvellous blend of Chinese vegetables and nuts,
stir-fried in a little oil and then cooked in an aromatic sauce.*

*SERVES 4*

2 dried lotus roots, soaked overnight in
 water
30ml/2 tbsps oil
75g/3oz bean sprouts
½ red pepper, seeded and finely chopped
½ green pepper, seeded and finely
 chopped
½ spring onion, chopped
1 head Chinese cabbage, finely chopped
75g/3oz dried Chinese black mushrooms,
 soaked for 1 hour in warm water
1 courgette thinly sliced
100g/4oz frozen peas
30g/2 tbsps cashew nuts, roughly
 chopped
5g/1 tsp sugar
30ml/2 tbsps soy sauce
430ml/¾ pint chicken stock
Salt and pepper

1. Cook the lotus roots in boiling, lightly salted water for 20 minutes. Slice thinly.

2. Heat the oil in a wok and stir-fry, in the following order, the bean sprouts peppers, onion, Chinese cabbage, lotus root, mushrooms, courgette, peas and cashew nuts.

3. Stir in the sugar, soy sauce and stock.

4. Season with salt and pepper and cook for 30 minutes, stirring frequently.

5. Serve the vegetables slightly drained of the sauce.

TIME: Preparation takes about 10 minutes and cooking takes approximately 35 minutes.

VARIATION: Any type of nut could be used in this recipe, for example walnuts, hazelnuts or almonds.

COOK'S TIP: If time permits, this recipe is even more delicious if the vegetables are stir-fried separately, each cooked vegetable being removed from the wok before continuing with the next. Finish by cooking all the vegetables together for 30 minutes in the chicken stock as above.

# SPECIAL MIXED VEGETABLES

*This dish illustrates the basic stir-frying technique for vegetables.*

*SERVES 4*

15ml/1 tbsp oil
1 clove garlic, crushed
2.5cm/1-inch piece fresh ginger, sliced
4 Chinese leaves, shredded
50g/2oz flat mushrooms, thinly sliced
50g/2oz bamboo shoots, sliced
3 sticks celery, diagonally sliced
60g/2oz baby corn, cut in half if large
1 small red pepper, cored, seeded and
    thinly sliced
50g/2oz bean sprouts
Salt and pepper
30ml/2 tbsps light soy sauce
Dash sesame oil
3 tomatoes, peeled, seeded and quartered

1. Heat the oil in a wok and add the ingredients in the order given, reserving the soy sauce, sesame oil and tomatoes.

2. To make it easier to peel the tomatoes, remove the stems and place in boiling water for 5 seconds.

3. Remove from the boiling water with a draining spoon and place in a bowl of cold water. This will make the peels easier to remove. Cut out the core end using a small sharp knife.

4. Cut the tomatoes in half and then in quarters. Use a teaspoon or a serrated edged knife to remove the seeds and the cores.

5. Cook the vegetables for about 2 minutes. Stir in the soy sauce and sesame oil and add the tomatoes. Heat through for 30 seconds and serve immediately.

TIME: Preparation takes about 25 minutes, cooking takes about 2-3 minutes.

VARIATION: Other vegetables such as broccoli florets, cauliflower florets, mange tout, courgettes or French beans may be used.

SERVING IDEA: Serve as a side dish or as a vegetarian main dish with plain or fried rice.

# SWEET AND SOUR CABBAGE

*A tasty combination which suits cabbage perfectly.*

*SERVES 4*

450g/1lb white cabbage, shredded
½ tsp bicarbonate of soda
5g/1 tsp salt
10g/2 tsps sugar
15ml/1 tbsp oil

*Sauce*
30g/2 tbsps sugar
30ml/2 tbsps wine vinegar
225ml/8 fl oz chicken stock or water
Pinch of salt
15g/1 tbsp cornflour or arrowroot
Few drops red food colouring
5g/1 tsp tomato purée

1. Boil the cabbage in a large pan of water with the bicarbonate of soda, salt and sugar for 2-3 minutes. Drain the cabbage and discard the boiling water.

2. Keep the cabbage in cold water for 5 minutes. Drain and keep on one side.

3. Heat the wok and add the oil. Fry the cabbage until it is heated through. Remove on to a serving dish.

4. Combine the sauce ingredients, stir well, add to the wok and gently bring to the boil, stirring. Stir over the heat until the sauce thickens. Pour over the cabbage and serve immediately.

TIME: Preparation takes 10 minutes, cooking takes 10 minutes.

COOK'S TIP: The red food colouring is optional as it only accentuates the colour.

# Aubergines and Peppers Szechuan Style

*Authentic Szechuan food is fiery hot. Outside China,*
*restaurants often tone down the taste for Western palates.*

*SERVES 4*

1 large aubergine
75ml/5 tbsps oil
2 cloves garlic, crushed
2.5cm/1-inch piece fresh ginger, shredded
1 onion, cut into 2.5cm/1-inch pieces
1 small green pepper, seeded, cored and
  cut into 2.5cm/1-inch pieces
1 small red pepper, seeded, cored and cut
  into 2.5cm/1-inch pieces
1 red or green chilli, seeded, cored and
  cut into thin strips
100ml/4fl oz chicken or vegetable stock
5g/1 tsp sugar
5g/1 tsp vinegar
Pinch salt and pepper
5ml/1 tsp cornflour
15g/1 tbsp soy sauce
Dash sesame oil
Oil for cooking

1. Cut the aubergine in half and score the surface.

2. Sprinkle lightly with salt and leave to drain in a colander or on paper towels for 30 minutes.

3. After 30 minutes, squeeze the aubergine gently to extract any bitter juices and rinse thoroughly under cold water. Pat dry and cut the aubergine into 2.5cm/1-inch cubes.

4. Heat about 45ml/3 tbsps oil in a wok. Add the aubergine and stir-fry for about 4-5 minutes. It may be necessary to add more oil as the aubergine cooks. Remove from the wok and set aside.

5. Reheat the wok and add 30ml/2 tbsps oil. Add the garlic and ginger and stir-fry for 1 minute. Add the onion and stir-fry for 2 minutes. Add the green pepper, red pepper and chilli pepper and stir-fry for 1 minute. Return the aubergine to the wok along with the remaining ingredients.

6. Bring to the boil, stirring constantly, and cook until the sauce thickens and clears. Serve immediately.

TIME: Preparation takes about 30 minutes, cooking takes about 7-8 minutes.

COOK'S TIP: Lightly salting the aubergine will help draw out any bitterness.

SERVING IDEA: Serve as a vegetarian stir-fry dish with plain or fried rice.

# STIR-FRIED STICKY RICE

*Glutinous rice cooked with stir-fried mushrooms,
ginger and spring onions.*

*SERVES 4*

250g/9oz glutinous rice
30ml/2 tbsps oil
2 spring onions, chopped
½ onion, chopped
1 slice fresh ginger root
4 dried Chinese black mushrooms, soaked
   for 15 minutes in warm water, drained
   and sliced
Salt and pepper

1. Wash the rice in plenty of cold water and place it in a sieve. Pour 5½ cups boiling water over the rice.

2. Heat the oil in a wok and fry the spring onions, onion and ginger until golden brown.

3. Add the mushrooms and continue cooking, stirring and shaking the wok frequently.

4. Add the rice and stir well. Pour over enough water to cover the rice by ½ inch.

5. Cover and cook over a moderate heat until there is almost no liquid left. Reduce the heat and continue cooking until all the liquid has been absorbed. This takes approximately 20 minutes in total.

6. Add salt and pepper to taste, remove the slice of ginger, and serve immediately.

TIME: Preparation takes 5 minutes and cooking takes approximately 25 minutes.

VARIATION: Replace the water with beef stock to give the rice more flavour.

234

235

# Microwave

Chicken Corn Chowder with Almonds
Prawn and Lettuce Soup
Soup of Mushrooms and Peas
Shanghai Noodle Snack
Ham and Bean Fried Rice
Embroidered Crabmeat Balls
Prawns with Sweetcorn
Scallops in Pepper Sauce
Beef with Green Pepper, Tomato
and Black Beans
Szechuan Beef
Singapore Chicken
Chicken with Mange Tout
Duck with Pineapple
Empress Chicken
Chicken with Hoisin Sauce and Cashews
Sweet-Sour Cabbage
Ten Varieties of Beauty
Mange Tout with Water Chestnuts
Spicy Cucumbers
Ginger Broccoli

# CHICKEN CORN CHOWDER WITH ALMONDS

*Toasted almonds add a special flavour to this chowder.*

*SERVES 4*

2 x 225g/8oz cans creamed corn
1150ml/2 pints chicken stock
2 chicken breasts, finely chopped
30g/2 tbsps cornflour
30ml/2 tbsps rice wine
50g/2oz toasted almonds
Salt and pepper

**1.** Combine corn, stock and chicken in a large deep bowl.

**2.** Partially cover and cook 3-5 minutes or until chicken is nearly cooked.

**3.** Combine cornflour and rice wine and stir into the soup.

**4.** Cook 2-3 minutes to allow cornflour to thicken and clear.

**5.** Sprinkle with toasted almonds, season and serve.

TIME: Preparation takes 15 minutes, microwave cooking takes 5-8 minutes.

# PRAWN AND LETTUCE SOUP

*This unusual sounding recipe is wonderfully
tasty with its distinctly Chinese consistency.*

*SERVES 4*

100g/4oz rice
1150ml/2 pints hot chicken stock
1 piece fresh ginger root, grated
360g/12oz peeled prawns
1 small head lettuce, shredded
Salt

**1.** Put the rice, stock and ginger into a
large, deep bowl. Partially cover and cook
12 minutes on HIGH, stirring often.

**2.** Cook until the rice softens completely.

**3.** Add the prawns, lettuce and salt. Leave
the soup to stand, covered, for 5 minutes.
Prawns should heat through in the stock.

TIME: Preparation takes 10 minutes, microwave cooking takes 12 minutes
plus 5 minutes standing time.

COOK'S TIP: Use your favourite lettuce in this soup.

# SOUP OF MUSHROOMS AND PEAS

*Astoundingly simple this recipe is the perfect answer to a soup in a hurry.*

*SERVES 4*

12 dried Chinese mushrooms, soaked
 30 minutes
100g/4oz ham, shredded
1150ml/2 pints light stock
15ml/1 tbsp light soy sauce
225g/8oz fresh peas
Salt and pepper

1. Remove the stems and slice the mushrooms finely.

2. Combine with the remaining ingredients and cook 10 minutes on HIGH or until peas are just tender.

TIME: Preparation takes 15 minutes, microwave cooking takes 10 minutes.

BUYING GUIDE: Chinese mushrooms are available in delicatessens and good supermarkets.

# SHANGHAI NOODLE SNACK

*Crabmeat adds a touch of style to this tasty snack.*

*SERVES 6*

450g/1lb Chinese egg noodles
1150ml/2 pints boiling water

*Sauce*
30g/2 tbsps cornflour dissolved in 60ml/
    2 fl oz water
30ml/3 tbsps rice wine
15ml/1 tbsp light soy sauce
280ml/½ pint light stock
1 small piece ginger root, thinly sliced

4 spring onions, thinly sliced diagonally
Meat from one large crab or 1 x 180g/6oz
    package frozen or canned crabmeat

1. Cook the noodles in the boiling water
for 3 minutes on HIGH.

2. Leave to stand 5 minutes, covered,
while preparing the sauce.

3. Combine the sauce ingredients in a
deep bowl, stirring well to mix the
cornflour

4. Cook 2-3 minutes until the sauce
thickens and clears.

5. Add the onions and crab and cook 3
seconds on HIGH.

6. Drain the noodles well and toss with
the sauce to serve.

TIME: Preparation takes 15 minutes, microwave cooking takes 5-6 minutes
plus 5 minutes standing time.

COOK'S TIP: Egg noodles are available in different thicknesses, choose the
thicker variety for this dish.

# HAM AND BEAN FRIED RICE

*The perfect side dish or lunch time snack.*

*SERVE 4*

---

45ml/3 tbsps oil
2 eggs, beaten
100g/4oz ham, chopped
225g/8oz cooked rice
100g/4oz green beans, cut in thin,
  diagonal slices
15ml/1 tbsp soy sauce
4 spring onions, chopped
Salt and pepper

---

**1.** Heat a browning dish 5 minutes on HIGH.

**2.** Pour in half the oil and half the beaten egg and cook for 30 seconds on HIGH on one side.

**3.** Turn over and cook for 30 seconds on the second side.

**4.** Keep the egg warm and add the remaining oil to the dish.

**5.** Heat for 1 minute on HIGH and add the ham. Cover the dish and cook for 1 minute on HIGH.

**6.** Add the rice and cook, covered, for 5 minutes on HIGH.

**7.** Add the beans, soy sauce, onions and seasoning. Cook 1 minute on HIGH and toss the ingredients to mix well.

**8.** Slice the eggs into thin strips and scatter over the top of the rice. Cover the dish and leave to stand for 2 minutes before serving.

---

TIME: Preparation takes 15 minutes, microwave cooking takes 9 minutes plus 2 minutes standing time.

VARIATION: Substitute other vegetables such as mushrooms for the green beans.

# EMBROIDERED CRABMEAT BALLS

*A wonderful combination of many much-loved Chinese ingredients.*

*SERVES 4-6*

450g/1lb crabmeat
2-3 eggs
5ml/1 tsp salt
Pinch pepper
15ml/1 tbsp sherry
15ml/1 tbsp cornflour
½ green pepper, finely chopped
¼ red pepper, finely chopped
30ml/2 tbsps finely chopped ham
2 spring onions, finely chopped
3 large Chinese leaves
2.5ml/½ tsp ground ginger
280ml/½ pint hot chicken stock
30g/2 tbsps cornflour
30ml/2 tbsps light soy sauce
Dash sesame oil

1. Mix the first 11 ingredients, adding only 2 egg whites. If the mixture is dry and crumbly, add some of the remaining white until the mixture will hold together.

2. Shape into 2.5cm/1-inch balls. The balls should not be smooth. Place in a single layer in a large shallow dish.

3. Pour around the hot stock and cover the dish. Cook 3 minutes on HIGH, rearranging the balls once during cooking to bring the ones in the centre of the dish to the outside. Remove the balls and keep warm.

4. Mix the remaining cornflour with the soy sauce in glass measure and gradually add the stock. Stir well and cook 2-3 minutes on HIGH, until thickened. Add the sesame oil and pour over the crabmeat balls to serve.

TIME: Preparation takes 25 minutes, microwave cooking takes 5-6 minutes.

# Prawns with Sweetcorn

*An old favourite which tastes great using*
*an up-to-date cooking method.*

*SERVES 4*

675g/1½lbs shelled king prawns,
  uncooked
45ml/3 tbsps oil
1 clove garlic, minced
1 small piece ginger root, minced
60ml/4 tbsps light stock
60ml/4 tbsps light soy sauce
60ml/4 tbsps rice wine
10g/2 tsps cornflour
30g/2 tbsps Chinese parsley (coriander
  leaves)
50g/2oz mange tout
100g/4oz baby ears of corn
Salt

**1.** Heat a browning dish for 5 minutes on HIGH.

**2.** Shell and de-vein the prawns if necessary. Add the oil to the dish and the prawns.

**3.** Add the garlic and ginger and cook for 1-2 minutes on HIGH, stirring often.

**4.** Combine the stock, soy sauce, wine and cornflour. Pour over the prawns, and cook for 3-4 minutes on MEDIUM, stirring halfway through the cooking time.

**5.** Cut the stalks off the mange tout and add with the ears of corn to the dish. Cut the corn in half lengthwise if the ears are large. Cook for 1-2 minutes on MEDIUM, until the sauce thickens and clears.

**6.** If the prawns are cooked after 3-4 minutes, remove them before adding the vegetables. Sprinkle with Chinese parsley before serving.

TIME: Preparation takes 20 minutes, microwave cooking takes 5-8 minutes.

COOK'S TIP: If you buy the prawns from a fishmonger they are often fresher than their supermarket equivalent.

# SCALLOPS IN PEPPER SAUCE

*Give your guests a treat with this special dish.*

*SERVE 4*

450g/1lb scallops, shelled and cleaned
½ clove garlic, finely chopped
45ml/3 tbsps rice wine
45ml/3 tbsps light soy sauce
Pinch sugar
Salt and pepper
15/1 tbsp cornflour dissolved in 90ml/
   3 fl oz light stock
60ml/4 tbsps sweet chilli sauce
1 small piece fresh ginger root, peeled and
   chopped
1 green pepper, thinly sliced
4 spring onions, sliced or shredded

**1.** If the scallops are large, cut in half, horizontally. Place in a casserole dish with the garlic, wine, soy sauce, sugar and salt and pepper.

**2.** Cover the dish and cook for 10 minutes on MEDIUM.

**3.** Remove the scallops and keep warm.

**4.** Add the cornflour and stock to the hot liquid and stir well. Add the chilli sauce and ginger root and cook 2-3 minutes, or until thickened.

**5.** Add the green pepper and onions to the sauce and return the scallops to the dish. Cook 1-2 minutes on HIGH, until the scallops are cooked and the vegetables are still crisp. Serve with rice.

TIME: Preparation takes 20 minutes, microwave cooking takes 13-15 minutes.

# BEEF WITH GREEN PEPPER, TOMATO AND BLACK BEANS

*Rump steak is needed for this recipe because of the
quick cooking – cheaper cuts of meat would be too tough.*

*SERVES 4*

450g/1lb rump steak, cut into thin slices
60ml/4 tbsps soy sauce
10ml/2 tsps dry sherry or rice wine

*Sauce*
45ml/3 tbsps salted black beans
30ml/3 tbsps water
280ml/8 fl oz brown stock
15g/1 tbsp sugar
30ml/3 tbsps cornflour dissolved in the
  stock
1 clove garlic, finely minced
1 large green pepper, cut in 2.1cm/1-inch
  pieces

3 tomatoes, peeled and quartered
Salt and pepper

**1.** Mix the steak, soy sauce and wine and
leave to marinate, covered, in the
refrigerator for 30 minutes.

**2.** Crush the black beans and mix with the
water. Leave to stand until ready to use.

**3.** Combine all the ingredients in a shallow
dish, except for the pepper and tomatoes.
Cover the dish and cook on HIGH 7-9
minutes, stirring halfway through the
cooking time.

**4.** Once the sauce has cleared, add the
pepper and tomatoes and cook 1 minute
further on HIGH.

TIME: Preparation takes 30 minutes, microwave cooking takes 8-10 minutes.

SERVING IDEA: Serve this dish with plain rice and garnish with spring onions.

# SZECHUAN BEEF

*This simple recipe brings out the flavour of the beef.*

*SERVES 4*

450g/1lb rump steak, shredded
30ml/2 tbsps oil
½ dried chilli pepper, crushed
60ml/4 tbsps soy sauce
100ml/4 fl oz stock
30g/2 tbsps cornflour
3 sticks celery, shredded
1 sweet red pepper, shredded

**1.** Heat a browning dish for 5 minutes on HIGH.

**2.** Combine meat and oil and add to the dish. Cook 2 minutes on HIGH in 2 or 3 batches. Re-heat browning dish 2 minutes after each batch.

**3.** Add the crushed chilli pepper.

**4.** Mix the soy sauce and stock and gradually stir into the cornflour. Pour over the steak and cook 2-3 minutes.

**5.** Add the celery and red pepper and mix together with the meat and sauce.

**6.** Cook a further 1 minute on HIGH until the sauce has thickened but the vegetables are still crisp.

TIME: Preparation takes 20 minutes, microwave cooking takes 6-18 minute.

COOK'S TIP: Do not substitute a cheaper cut of meat or the final result will be Tough Beef!

256

# SINGAPORE CHICKEN

*Chicken, pineapple and mandarin*
*form the basis of this colourful dish.*

*SERVES 4*

30ml/2 tbsps oil
10g/2 tsps curry powder
450g/1lb chicken, skinned, boned and cut
  into bite-sized pieces
1 large onion, cut in large pieces
15g/1 tbsp cornflour
1 x 230g/8oz can pineapple chunks, juice
  reserved
1 x 300g/10oz can mandarin orange
  segments, juice reserved
50g/2oz bean sprouts
Dash soy sauce
Salt and pepper

1. Heat the oil in a large casserole dish for
30 seconds on HIGH.

2. Add the curry powder, and cook 30
seconds on HIGH.

3. Add the chicken, cover the dish and
cook 5 minutes on HIGH.

4. Add the onion, mix the cornflour with
the reserved pineapple and orange juice
and add to the chicken. Cover and cook 5
minutes on HIGH, stirring occasionally
after 1 minute.

5. When the sauce thickens, add the
pineapple, orange segments and bean
sprouts.

6. Leave to stand 2 minutes before serving.
Serve with fried or plain boiled rice.

Time: Preparation takes 20 minutes, microwave cooking takes 11 minutes
plus 2 minutes standing time.

Cook's Tip: Do not buy the bean sprout too far in advance as they deteriorate rapidly.

# CHICKEN WITH MANGE TOUT

*Mange tout brings a flavour all its own to any recipe.*

*SERVES 4*

30ml/2 tbsps oil
450g/1lb chicken breasts, skinned, boned
   and cut into thin slivers
10g/2 tsps cornflour
45ml/3 tbsps rice wine
45ml/3 tbsps light soy sauce
30ml/2 tbsps oyster sauce
60ml/4 tbsps chicken stock
Dash sesame oil
Salt and pepper
100g/4oz mange tout

1. Heat the oil 30 seconds on HIGH in a large casserole dish.

2. Mix the remaining ingredients except the mange tout, and pour over the chicken.

3. Cover and cook 7-9 minutes on HIGH, stirring halfway through cooking time.

4. Add the mange tout, re-cover the dish and cook 30 seconds on HIGH.

5. Leave to stand for 2 minutes before serving. Serve with rice.

TIME: Preparation takes 20 minutes, microwave cooking takes 8½-9½minutes plus 2 minutes standing time.

BUYING GUIDE: Oyster sauce is a common ingredients in Chinese cooking and is widely available in supermarkets.

# DUCK WITH PINEAPPLE

*A great combination that always goes down well.*

*SERVES 4*

*Sauce*
225g/8oz can crushed pineapple, or
    1 fresh pineapple, peeled and cored
7.5ml/1½ tsps cornflour dissolved in
    15ml/1 tbsp water
15ml/1 tbsp light soy sauce
7.5ml/1½ tsps sugar
15ml/1 tbsp white wine
1 piece ginger root, grated
Pinch salt

2.5kg/5lb duckling
30ml/2 tbsps oil
30ml/2 tbsps soy sauce

*Garnish*
4 chives, shredded

1. If using fresh pineapple, work in a food processor until finely chopped. Add remaining sauce ingredients and mix well in a small, deep bowl. Cook 4 minutes on HIGH until the sauce thickens and clears.

2. Skin the duck and remove the leg and breast meat. Cut into thin slivers.

3. Heat a browning dish 5 minutes on HIGH. Toss the oil and duck together, and add to the browning dish. Cook, uncovered, 4 minutes on HIGH.

4. Add the soy sauce, cover the dish and reduce the setting to MEDIUM. Cook a further 3 minutes or until duck is tender.

5. Remove duck to a serving dish and keep warm. Coat with the pineapple sauce and sprinkle on the chives. Serve with rice.

TIME: Preparation takes 20 minutes, microwave cooking takes 9-10 minutes.

# EMPRESS CHICKEN

*As its name suggests this is a special dish fit for any guest.*

*SERVES 4*

4 chicken wings
4 chicken breasts, skinned
12 dried Chinese mushrooms
100ml/4 fl oz soy sauce
570ml/1 pint chicken stock mixed with
    45ml/3 tbsps cornflour
15g/1 tbsp sugar
2 pieces star anise
2 slices ginger root
15ml/1 tbsp rice wine
½ tsp salt
2 can bamboo shoots, drained and cut in
    strips if thick
4 spring onions, sliced

**1.** With a heavy clever, chop the chicken, through the bones, into large chunks. Remove any splinters of bone.

**2.** Soak the mushrooms in hot water for 30 minutes. Drain and trim off the stems.

**3.** Put the chicken, mushrooms and remaining ingredients, except the onions and bamboo shoots, into a deep casserole.

**4.** Cover well and cook 15 minutes on HIGH or until the chicken is completely cooked.

**5.** Add the bamboo shoots and sliced onions. Leave to stand 3 minutes and remove star anise before serving.

TIME: Preparation takes 30 minutes, microwave cooking takes 15 minutes plus 3 minutes standing time.

COOK'S TIP: Dried Chinese mushrooms have a very distinctive flavour so only substitute fresh mushrooms as a last resort.

# CHICKEN WITH HOISIN SAUCE AND CASHEWS

*Cashews accentuate the taste of meat*
*whilst adding a delightful flavour.*

*SERVES 4*

450g/1lb chicken, skinned, boned and cut
   into bite-sized pieces
15g/1 tbsp cornflour
280ml/½ pint stock
15ml/1 tbsp light soy sauce
1 clove garlic, finely minced
1 tbsp white wine
60ml/4 tbsps Hoisin sauce
60g/2oz roasted cashew nuts
4 spring onions, diagonally sliced

1. Combine the chicken with all the
ingredients except the nuts and onions.

2. Put into a casserole dish, cover and
cook on HIGH for 7-9 minutes, stirring
halfway through the cooking time.

3. Once the sauce has thickened and the
cornflour has cleared, add the nuts and
the spring onions.

4. Re-cover the dish and leave to stand 2
minutes before serving. Serve with rice.

TIME: Preparation takes 20 minutes, microwave cooking takes 7-9 minutes
plus 2 minutes standing time.

COOK'S TIP: Ensure the cashew nuts are unsalted. If you can only
buy salted ones, rinse before using.

# Sweet-Sour Cabbage

*The perfect refreshing side dish.*

*SERVES 4*

1 medium head white cabbage, about
    900g/2lbs
1 small red chilli pepper (use less if
    desired)
100g/4oz light brown sugar
90ml/3 fl oz rice wine vinegar
30ml/2 tbsps light soy sauce
Salt
45ml/3 tbsps oil

**1.** Cut the cabbage into 1.25cm/½-inch slices, discarding the core. Cut the chilli pepper into thin, short strips, discarding the seeds.

**2.** Mix all the ingredients together except the oil.

**3.** Pour the oil into a large bowl and heat for 2 minutes on HIGH.

**4.** Add the cabbage and the liquid and cover the bowl with pierced cling film. Cook on HIGH for 9-11 minutes.

**5.** Allow to cool in the bowl, stirring frequently. When cold, refrigerate.

TIME: Preparation takes 20 minutes, microwave cooking takes 11-13 minutes.

COOK'S TIP: Vary the amount of sugar and chilli pepper according to your own taste.

269

# Ten Varieties of Beauty

*The name of this recipe refers to the variety
of vegetables in the recipe.*

*SERVES 4-6*

60ml/4 tbsps oil
3 sticks celery, diagonally sliced
2 carrots, peeled and cut into ribbons with
   a vegetable peeler
90g/3oz mange tout
1 red pepper, thickly sliced
8 ears of baby corn
4 spring onions, diagonally sliced
60g/2oz bean sprouts
10 water chestnuts, sliced
½ small can sliced bamboo shoots
10 Chinese dried mushrooms, soaked in
   hot water, stalks removed
280ml/½ pint chicken stock
30g/2 tbsps cornflour
45ml/3 tbsps light soy sauce
Sesame oil

1. Heat a browning dish for 5 minutes on
HIGH. Pour in the oil and add the celery
and carrots. Cook for 1 minute on HIGH.

2. Remove from the dish and add the
mange tout, red pepper and corn. Cook
for 1 minute on HIGH and place with the
celery and carrots.

3. Add the onions, bean sprouts, water
chestnuts and bamboo shoots to the dish.
Cook for 1 minute on HIGH, adding the
mushrooms after 30 seconds.

4. Place with the rest of vegetables.

5. Combine the rest of the ingredients in a
glass measure. Cook 2-3 minutes on HIGH
until thickened. Taste and add salt if
necessary. Pour over the vegetables and
stir carefully.

6. Reheat for 1-2 minutes on HIGH before
serving.

TIME: Preparation takes 20 minutes, microwave cooking takes 6-8 minutes.

# BEANS WITH BAMBOO SHOOTS

*An unusual combination which is wonderfully tasty.*

*SERVES 4*

6 pieces Chinese black fungi (tree or wood ears), soaked 30 minutes
225g/8oz green beans, cut into 2 inch diagonal pieces
2 whole pieces tinned bamboo shoots, cut into thin triangular pieces
2 tbsps oil
2 tbsps soy sauce
2 tsps cornflour
4 tbsps light stock and wine mixed
Dash sesame oil
Salt and pepper

1. Heat a browning dish for 5 minutes on HIGH. Pour in the oil and add the beans and bamboo shoots. Cook, uncovered, for 2 minutes on HIGH.
2. Add the tree ears, cover the dish and leave to stand while preparing the sauce.
3. Mix the remaining ingredients except the sesame oil in a glass measure. Cook for 2 minutes on HIGH, stirring once until thickened.
4. Combine with the vegetables and stir in the sesame oil to serve.

TIME: Preparation takes 30 minutes, microwave cooking takes 4 minutes.

# SPICY CUCUMBERS

*This refreshing side dish is perfect served with a spicy main course.*

*SERVES 4*

1 large cucumber
Salt
45ml/3 tbsps light soy sauce
Pinch five-spice powder
¼ tsp crushed red pepper
10ml/2 tsps sesame oil
15ml/1 tbsp rice vinegar
45ml/3 tbsps Chinese parsley leaves
   (coriander leaves)

**1.** Peel thin strips off the cucumber with a canelle knife for a white and green striped effect. Cut in half lengthwise, or in quarters if the cucumber is thick. Cut the lengths into 5cm/2-inch pieces. Sprinkle with salt and leave to stand 30 minutes.

**2.** Wash and dry well. Combine the cucumber with all the remaining ingredients, except the parsley, in a deep bowl. Partially cover and cook for 2 minutes on HIGH.

**3.** Add the parsley and leave in the bowl to cool. When cold, refrigerate. Serve on the same day.

TIME: Preparation takes 30 minutes, microwave cooking takes 2 minutes.

# GINGER BROCCOLI

*Ginger complements the taste of broccoli perfectly in this tasty side dish.*

*SERVES 4*

675g/1½lbs broccoli
30ml/2 tbsps oil
7.5cm/3-inch piece fresh ginger root,
    peeled and very finely shredded
Pinch salt
Pinch sugar
5ml/1 tsp cornflour
120ml/4 fl oz light stock
Dash light soy sauce

1. Heat a browning dish for 5 minutes on HIGH.

2. Cut off the tough ends of the broccoli stems.

3. Cut the flowerets from the stems in small clusters.

4. Peel the stems with a vegetable peeler and cut them into thin diagonal slices.

5. Pour the oil into the browning dish and add the broccoli stem slices.

6. Add the ginger and cook, uncovered, for 2 minutes on HIGH, stirring frequently.

7. Add the florets, cover and set aside while preparing the sauce.

8. Combine the remaining ingredients in a glass measure. Cook, uncovered, for 5-6 minutes on HIGH until thickened. Pour over the broccoli and stir together to serve.

TIME: Preparation takes 20 minutes, microwave cooking takes 7-8 minutes.

COOK'S TIP: Adding the broccoli florets after the stems have been cooked is just enough to lightly warm them.

# Sweets

Almond Float with Fruit
Kiwi and Coconut Duo
Spun Fruits
Peking Toffee Apples
Almond Cookies
Melon Salad
Chinese Bean Buns
Exotic Fruit Salad
Sweet Bean Wontons
Half-Moon Banana Pastries
Candied Apples

# ALMOND FLOAT WITH FRUIT

*Sweet dishes are not often served in the course of a Chinese meal. Banquets are the exception, and this elegant fruit salad is certainly special enough.*

*SERVES 6-8*

1 envelope unflavoured gelatine
90ml/6 tbsps cold water
90g/3oz sugar
280ml/½ pint milk
5ml/1 tsp almond essence
Few drops red or yellow food colouring
   (optional)

*Almond Sugar Syrup*
90g/3oz sugar
570ml/1 pint water
½ tsp almond essence
Fresh fruit such as kiwi, mango,
   pineapple, bananas, lychees, oranges or
   satsumas, peaches, berries, cherries,
   grapes or starfruit
Fresh mint for garnish

1. Allow the gelatine to soften in the cold water for about 10 minutes or until spongy. Put in a large mixing bowl.

2. Bring 180ml/6 fl oz water to the boil and stir in the sugar. Pour into the gelatine and water mixture and stir until gelatine and sugar dissolves.

3. Add milk, 1 tsp almond essence and food colouring if using. Mix well and pour into a 20cm/8-inch square pan. Chill in the refrigerator until set.

4. Mix the sugar and water for the syrup together in a heavy-based pan. Cook over gentle heat until the sugar dissolves. Bring to the boil and allow to boil for about 2 minutes, or until the syrup thickens slightly. Add the almond essence and allow to cool at room temperature. Chill in the refrigerator until ready to use.

5. Prepare the fruit and place in attractive serving dish. Pour over the chilled syrup and mix well.

6. Cut the set almond float into 2.5cm/1 inch diamond shapes or cubes. Use a spatula to remove them from the pan and stir them gently into the fruit mixture. Decorate with sprigs of fresh mint to serve.

TIME: Preparation takes about 25 minutes. The almond float will need about 2 hours to set.

PREPARATION: To prepare kiwi fruit, peel with a swivel vegetable peeler and cut into thin rounds. To prepare lychees, peel and cut into thin slices around the large stone. To prepare starfruit, wash and cut crosswise into thin slices. The shape of the slices will resemble a star.

BUYING GUIDE: Use whatever fruits are in season at the moment, or use good quality canned fruit. Exotic fruits are avilable in most large supermarket and some greengrocers. Allow about 900g/2lbs of fruit for 6-8 people.

# KIWI AND COCONUT DUO

*Incredibly simple to prepare, this recipe is a delicious blend of kiwi fruit, fresh coconut and coconut milk.*

*SERVES 4*

4 kiwi fruit
1 fresh coconut
A little sugar (optional)

1. Remove the stalks from the ends of the kiwis.

2. Peel them lengthwise with a small sharp knife.

3. Slice them thinly widthways.

4. Cut the coconut into pieces, reserving all the milk.

5. Cut the coconut flesh into very thin slices.

6. Arrange the kiwi slices on a serving plate and surround with the slices of coconut.

7. Add a little sugar to the coconut milk if desired and pour over the fruit. Serve chilled.

TIME: Preparation takes about 25 minutes.

VARIATION: Coconut milk can now be bought in cans. It is usually of very high quality and is thicker than fresh coconut milk.

COOK'S TIP: The addition of sugar to the milk is optional, and depends upon the acidity of the milk.

# SPUN FRUITS

*Often called toffee fruits, this sweet consists of fruit
fried in batter and coated with a thin, crisp caramel glaze.*

*SERVES 4*

*Batter*
100g/4oz plain flour, sifted
Pinch salt
1 egg
140ml/¼ pint water and milk mixed half
    and half
Oil for deep frying

*Caramel Syrup*
225g/8oz sugar
45ml/3 tbsps water
15ml/1 tbsp oil

1 large apple, peeled, cored and cut into
    5cm/2-inch chunks
1 banana, peeled and cut into 2.5cm/
    1-inch pieces
Ice water

1. To prepare the batter, combine all the batter ingredients, except the oil for deep frying, in a liquidizer or food processor and process to blend. Pour into a bowl and dip in the prepared fruit.

2. In a heavy-based saucepan, combine the sugar with the water and oil and cook over very low heat until the sugar dissolves. Bring to the boil and allow to cook rapidly until a pale caramel colour.

3. While the sugar is dissolving heat the oil in a wok and fry the batter-dipped fruit, a few pieces at a time.

4. While the fruit is still hot and crisp use chopsticks or a pair of tongs to dip the fruit into the hot caramel syrups. Stir each piece around to coat evenly.

5. Dip immediately into ice water to harden the syrup and place each piece on a greased dish. Continue cooking all the fruit in the same way.

6. Once the caramel has hardened and the fruit has cooled, transfer to a clean serving plate.

TIME: Preparation takes about 25 minutes, cooking takes from 10-15 minutes.

VARIATION: Lychees may be used. Organisation is very important for the success of this dish. Have the batter ready, syrup prepared, fruit sliced and ice water on hand before beginning.

WATCHPOINT: Watch the syrup carefully and do not allow it to become too brown.

# PEKING TOFFEE APPLES

*A quick and easy sweet to prepare and one which you never grow out of!*

*SERVES 4*

4 crisp apples
1 egg
50g/2oz flour
Oil for deep frying
90g/6 tbsps sugar
45ml/3 tbsps oil
45ml/3 tbsps syrup

1. Peel, core and thickly slice the apples.

2. Blend the egg, flour and 60ml/2 fl oz water to make a smooth batter.

3. Dip each piece of apple in the batter.

4. Deep fry the apple in the oil for 2-3 minutes. Drain.

5. Heat the sugar, oil and 2 tbsps water in a pan over a low heat for 5 minutes.

6. Add the syrup, stir for a further 2 minutes.

7. Add the apple pieces and stir slowly, covering each piece of apple with syrup.

8. Quickly spoon hot, syrup-covered apples into a large bowl of iced water to harden syrup. Remove quickly and serve.

TIME: Preparation takes 10 minutes, cooking takes 10 minutes.

# ALMOND COOKIES

*In China these biscuits are often eaten as a between-meal snack. In Western-style cuisine, they make a good accompaniment to fruit or sorbet.*

*MAKES 30 COOKIES*

100g/4oz butter or margarine
60g/4 tbsps caster sugar
30g/2 tbsps light brown sugar
1 egg, beaten
Almond essence
100g/4oz plain flour
5g/1 tsp baking powder
Pinch salt
30g/1oz ground almonds, blanched or
   unblanched
30ml/2 tbsps water
30 whole blanched almonds

**1.** Cream the butter or margarine together with the two sugars until light and fluffy.

**2.** Divide the beaten egg in half and add half to the sugar mixture with a few drops of the almond essence and beat until smooth. Reserve the remaining egg for later use. Sift the flour, baking powder and salt into the egg mixture and add the ground almonds. Stir well by hand.

**3.** Shape the mixture into small balls and place well apart on a lightly greased baking sheet. Flatten slightly and press an almond on to the top of each one.

**4.** Mix the reserved egg with the water and brush each cookie before baking.

**5.** Place in a preheated 180°C/350°F/Gas mark 4 oven and bake for 12-15 minutes. Cookies will be a pale golden colour when done.

TIME: Preparation takes about 10 minutes. If the dough becomes too soft, refrigerate for 10 minutes before shaping. Cooking takes about 12-15 minutes per batch.

COOK'S TIP: Roll the mixture on a floured surface with floured hands to prevent sticking.

WATCHPOINT: Do not over beat once the almonds are added. They will begin to oil and the mixture will become too soft and sticky to shape.

SERVING IDEA: Serve with fruit, ice cream or sorbet.

FREEZING: Cookies may be frozen baked or unbaked. Defrost uncooked dough completely at room temperature before baking. Baked cookies may be re-crisped by heating in the oven for about 2 minutes and then allowed to cool before serving.

# MELON SALAD

*A refreshing fruit salad, which is especially tasty
served after a heavy meal of many courses.*

*SERVES 4*

1 large cantaloupe melon
1 mango
4 canned lychees
4 large or 8 small strawberries
Lychee syrup from the can

**1.** Peel and seed the melon and cut into thin slices.

**2.** Peel and pit the mango and cut into thin slices.

**3.** Using a melon baller, cut as many balls as possible out the strawberries.

**4.** Arrange the melon slices evenly on 4 small plates.

**5.** Spread a layer of mango over the melon. Place a lychee in the centre of each plate and arrange a few strawberry balls around the edges.

**6.** Divide the lychee syrup evenly between the plates of fruit and chill them in the refrigerator before serving.

TIME: Preparation takes about 30 minutes.

VARIATION: Use a honeydew melon instead of the cantaloupe variety.

COOK'S TIP: This dessert is best served well chilled from the refrigerator, so prepare it several hours in advance of serving.

# CHINESE BEAN BUNS

*The Chinese do not often eat sweets but this one is a favourite.*

*MAKES 12-14*

60ml/2 fl oz milk
50g/2oz sugar
½ tsp salt
25g/1oz lard
50ml/2 fl oz warm water
10g/2 tsps dried yeast
1 egg, beaten
275g/8oz plain flour

*Filling*
100g/4oz sweet bean paste
25g/1oz sugar
25g/1oz chopped walnuts
15g/1 tbsp lard

1. Bring the milk almost to the boil. Stir in the sugar, salt and lard. Cool slightly.

2. Put the warm water and yeast into a bowl and stir to mix. Add the lukewarm milk mixture.

3. Add the beaten egg and 225g/8oz of the flour and beat until smooth.

4. Add the remaining flour and mix to a dough. Turn dough out onto a well-floured board and knead until smooth and elastic. Place in a greased bowl. Brush the dough with oil and cover. Leave to rise in a warm place until doubled in size (about 1 hour).

5. Heat the filling ingredients together in a wok for 5-6 minutes until smooth and shiny. Remove and cool. Divide the filling into 12-14 portions.

6. Knead the risen dough again for 2 minutes and then divide the dough into 12-14 portions. Flatten into thick circular shapes 10cm/4 inches in diameter. Place a chopstick on each circle of dough to market it in half, and then in half again. Cut along the marks to within 1/3 of the centre.

7. Place one portion of filling in the centre of the dough circle and fold the cut ends in to meet in the centre, to form a rosette. Secure by pinching ends of dough together.

8. Place a piece of greased foil over the pinched ends and place the buns on a greased baking tray. Brush with a little milk. Bake at 190°C/375°F/Gas Mark 5 for 20-25 minutes.

TIME: Preparation takes about 2 hours, including proving time, cooking takes about 30 minutes.

# EXOTIC FRUIT SALAD

*Fresh fruit marinated in orange and lychee juice with just a hint of almond.*

*SERVES 4*

1 papaya
1 pomegranate
2 kiwi fruit
4 rambutan fruit
4 canned lychees, plus the juice from the can
3 blood oranges
3 drops bitter almond extract, or ordinary almond extract

**1.** Peel all the fruit except the oranges, removing pips or pitting each fruit as necessary. Try to buy a fully ripe papaya for the salad. Cut it in half. Using a small spoon, remove all the pips and any stringy skin around them. Peel each half, but not too thickly as the flesh immediately below the skin is very good. Finally, cut the flesh into thin slices or other fancy shapes.

**2.** Peel two of the oranges. Remove all the pith and cut the flesh into small pieces.

**3.** Squeeze the juice from the remaining orange, mix this with the canned lychee juice and add the almond extract.

**4.** Cut all the remaining fruit into slices, rounds or small cubes and combine these with the prepared papaya and oranges in a bowl. Pour over the almond flavoured juices and leave the salad to marinate for a few hours in the refrigerator.

**5.** Serve chilled.

TIME: Prepration takes about 1 hour and the salad should be left to marinate for at least 3 hours.

SERVING IDEA: Cut a few fresh mint leaves into thin strips to garnish the fruit salad just before serving.

WATCHPOINT: Exotic fruit often arrives in the ships before it is ripe. The solution is to sweeten the sauce slightly before marinating the fruit in order to eliminate acidity.

BUYING GUIDE: If any of the fruits are out of season and unavailable, substitute other appropriate fruit, as desired.

# Sweet Bean Wontons

*Wonton snacks, either sweet or savoury, are another popular
tea house treat. Made from prepared wonton wrappers and
ready-made bean paste, they couldn't be more simple.*

*SERVES 6*

15 wonton wrappers
225g/8oz sweet red bean paste
15g/1 tbsp cornflour
60ml/4 tbsps cold water
Oil for deep frying
Honey

**1.** Take wonton wrapper in the palm of your hand and place a little of the red bean paste slightly above the centre.

**2.** Mix together the cornflour and water and moisten the edge around the filling.

**3.** Fold over, slightly off centre.

**4.** Pull the sides together, using the cornflour and water paste to stick the two together.

**5.** Turn inside out by gently pushing the filled centre.

**6.** Heat enough oil in a wok for deep-fat frying and when hot, put in 4 of the filled wontons at a time. Cook until crisp and golden and remove to paper towels to drain. Repeat with the remaining filled wontons. Served drizzled with honey.

VARIATION: Add a small amount of grated ginger to the red bean paste for a slight change in flavour. Wontons may also be sprinkled with sugar instead of honey.

BUYING GUIDE: Wontons, wonton wrappers and red bean paste are available in Chinese supermarkets.

# HALF-MOON BANANA PASTRIES

*These crunchy pastries are rather dry, and are*
*traditionally served with a cup of Chinese tea.*

*SERVES 4*

*Pastry Dough*
100g/4oz margarine
450g/1lb plain flour, sifted
Pinch salt
140ml/¼ pint water

*Filling*
3 bananas
10g/2 tsps sugar
Pinch cinnamon
Few drops of lemon juice
1 egg yolk, beaten

**1.** Cut the margarine into the flour and salt. Using your fingers, incorporate the water gradually to form a ball. Wrap a damp cloth around the dough and leave it to rest in a cool place for 30 minutes.

**2.** Peel and crush the bananas with a fork. Add the sugar, cinnamon and lemon juice. Mix together well.

**3.** Roll out small pieces of dough on a lightly floured surface and cut into circles. Place a little of the banana filling on each round of dough. Fold into half-moon shapes and seal the edges first by pinching together with your fingers and then by decorating with a fork.

**4.** Continue until all the dough and filling have been used.

**5.** Brush the beaten egg yolk over the half-moon pastries. Pierce the pastries once to allow steam to escape during cooking. Cook in a moderate oven, 180°C/350°F/Gas Mark 4, for approximately 20 minutes, until crisp and golden.

TIME: Preparation takes about 25 minutes, resting time for the dough is 30 minutes and cooking takes approximately 20 minutes.

VARIATION: Make up the pastries using different fruit fillings.

COOK'S TIP: The cooked dough in this recipe is very crisp. Serve the pastries with a fruit drink in summer and hot Chinese tea in winter.

WATCHPOINT: Be sure to seal the edges of the pastries thoroughly so that no filling escapes during cooking.

# CANDIED APPLES

*Candied fruit recipes are popular in Chinese cuisine.*
*This one is extra special with a rich batter, and*
*delicious sesame seeds to garnish.*

*SERVES 4*

3 cooking apples
1150ml/2 pints fresh oil
430ml/¾pint sesame oil
100g/4oz sugar
15g/1 tbsp toasted sesame seeds

*Batter*
2 eggs
40g/1½oz flour
40g/1½oz cornflour
Ice water

1. Peel and core the apples and cut into thick circles.

2. Mix the batter ingredients together to make a smooth, thick batter adding water as necessary.

3. Dip the apples in flour and then into the batter.

4. Mix the two oils together and heat to moderate. Deep-fry the apples slices for about 1 minute. Drain and set aside.

5. Heat the oil until it is hot, then fry the apple slices again, for about 40 seconds. This will make them nice and crisp.

6. Pour off most of the oil used to fry the apples, leaving about 3 tablespoons. Add the sugar to this and stir over high heat until the sugar caramelises. Add the apple slices and sesame seeds and stir to coat evenly then remove.

7. Dip the slices into ice cold water to set the syrup before serving.

TIME: Preparation takes about 10 minutes, cooking takes 5 minutes.

# Glossary

## Bean Pastes

Sauces made from soya beans. There are many varieties of bean paste. Hot bean paste, which is made with chillies and is salty. Soy Bean Paste, which is dark in colour, very salty and is made with fermented soya beans. Sweet Bean Paste, which is made with black soya beans, sugar flour and spices. Yellow Bean Paste, which is made with Yellow Soya Beans, is also quite salty in taste.

## Bean Sprouts

These are the shoots of mung beans or soya beans. They are readily available from most supermarkets. Although beans sprouts will keep for about a day in a perforated plastic bag it is best to buy them on the day of use.

## Black Bean Sauce

This can be bought ready-made from shops or made with 3-4 tbsps steamed black soya beans mixed to a paste with 2 tbsps oil and 2 tbsps sugar.

## Chilli Sauce

This is a very hot and tangy sauce made from chillies and vinegar. Chilli sauce can be easily purchased from many supermarkets and all Chinese grocers. It is used to season a wide variety of savoury Chinese dishes.

## Chillies

There are numerous varieties of chillies varying in size and strength of flavour. Commonly used in Eastern cooking are the red and green finger-like chillies about 4-inches long, and the tiny red and green bird's eye chillies which are very hot.

When preparing chillies it is advisable to wear rubber gloves and avoid getting the oils near lips or eyes. The seeds, which are very hot, should be discarded unless a fiery dish is required.

## Chinese Cabbage

There are two main varieties, Pak-choy and Choy-sum. These are sometimes available in supermarkets and vegetable markets as well as Chinese grocers. Chinese leaves, on the other hand, are available in most supermarkets. All these cabbages can be substituted by ordinary cabbage.

## Chinese Parsley

Otherwise known as fresh coriander, this is a herb of Indian origin, which is used as a flavouring and a garnish. The flat leaves have a strong flavour and cannot be substituted by Western parsley.

## Chinese Wine

There are many kinds of wine made from rice, Shao Hsing and Japanese Sake are two of the most popular and one can be substituted for the other. If you cannot obtain either of these dry sherry is a good substitute.

## Cloud Ear

This is known by many names e.g.. wood ear, snow fungus, sea jelly or jelly sheet. It is actually a dried fungus which when soaked in water, resembles a puffed ear, hence the name. It has no flavour and is used only to add texture to a dish. They are available in Chinese grocers.

## Cooked Oil

This is oil which has been used at least once before and therefore has a richer flavour than new cooking oil. If you wish to use new oil, heat it until it smokes before using.

## Five-Spice Powder

This is a blend of cinnamon, cloves, star anise, fennel and brown peppercorns. The mixture is often used to marinate meat or poultry.

## Ginger

The root stem of this plant can be purchased whole, sliced or ground, but it is always best to use fresh ginger and chop or grate as needed. Ginger is a vital ingredient in Chinese cooking as nearly all traditional meat and fish dishes use root ginger.

## Hoisin Sauce

This is a brownish-red sauce made from soya beans, salt, chilli, sugar, garlic, vinegar and flour. It has a sweet, tangy flavour and can be bought from Chinese or large supermarkets. It is used in cooking as well as being served as a dip for meats etc.

**Maltose**
A molasses-like substance which is made by fermenting barley or a similar grain. It can be substituted in recipes by honey, golden syrup or treacle.

**Monosodium Glutamate**
This is a white crytalline substance used extensively in Chinese cooking for tenderising meat and enhancing the flavour of dishes. It should be used sparingly as too much will spoil the dish. It can be totally omitted without unduly altering the taste of a dish.

**Dried Mushrooms**
Tree Fungus found in the East on oak logs and Shii trees. They are sold dried and have to be reconstituted by soaking in hot water. They are expensive, but only a few are needed to impart their distinctive woody flavour to a dish.

**Noodles**
There are many different kinds of noodles. Some are made from wheat flour, some from rice flour and some from bean flour. Egg noodles can be either thin or thick. The thin noodles are sold in 'cakes' whereas the thick noodles are spaghetti like and are often called Shanghai noodles. Bean Thread noodles are thin, white noodles which go transparent when cooked. They are mostly used in soups and stews and should be soaked before use. Rice Stick noodles are very thin noodles.

**Oyster Sauce**
This is a special sauce produced from soy sauce and oysters which have been fermented together. It is now widely available in supermarkets.

**Rice**
There are many different varieties of rice. Long grained rice is the variety usually used for making simple rice dishes. Basmati is the finest and most expensive long-grain rice. Glutinous rice is also common in Chinese cooking. It is a medium-grain rice used for making puddings and savoury dishes.

**Sesame Oil**
An aromatic oil produced from sesame seeds. This has a special flavour and is used as a seasoning and is a vital ingredient in some sauces. It is available from most good supermarkets.

**Soy Sauce**
There are two different types; one is

dark and the other is light. Both are used to flavouring nearly all Chinese foods. The dark soy sauce is stronger in flavour and thicker, whilst the light soy sauce is a weaker infusion.

**Star Anise**
This is an eight-pointed clove with a strong anise smell and flavour. It can be purchased as a powder or whole.

**Szechuan Pickle**
This salty pickle is made from cabbage, chillies and mustard and has a strong flavour. It is sold in jars and cans and is available from Chinese grocers.

**Water Chestnuts**
These are the bulb-like stems of the bulrush. They are slightly sweet and have a crisp texture.

# Index